# 10 STEPS TO CHANGING CAREERS

## BREAK FREE AND DO WORK YOU LOVE

### JEFF ALTMAN

# Table of Contents

Intruduction................................................... 1

Step 1: Self-Assessment - The Foundation of a Successful Career Transition . 2

Step 2: Define Your Goals and Let Them Guide You............... 16

Step 3:Networking: Forge Connections ......................... 21

Step 4: Do a Skill Gap Analysis ............................... 46

Step 5: Research Your New Career............................. 65

Step 6: Craft a Winning First Impression ....................... 84

Step 7: Mastering Your New Path: The Power of Continuous Learning  115

Step 8: Test Drive Your Future: Volunteer and Intern Experiences ... 143

Step 9: Mentorship: Your Career Transition Catalyst.............. 166

Step 10: Unlocking Career Doors Through Professional Associations  187

Epilogue To Sum Up........................................ 217

More from Jeff Altman ..................................... 219

# Intruduction

Are you stuck in a job that no longer fulfills you? Are you dreading each morning like clockwork? If you're nodding, it may be time for a career reboot.

Making a career transition can feel overwhelming - like staring into a void of uncertainty. But what if I told you there's a step-by-step roadmap to finding your new professional passion? One that avoids the pitfalls of hastily jumping ship without a plan?

As a career coach, I've guided professionals from many backgrounds through successful reinventions. I've witnessed the spark reignite when they finally land in the right role. In this book, you'll gain an insider's guide to researching and landing your dream career - one that goes far beyond the surface-level tips you'll uncover from a quick Google search. Packed with proven strategies and hard-won insights, this is your life raft for navigating the rocky waters of career transition. Brace yourself as we journey beyond your comfort zone and into enriching new possibilities. Your next career is out there waiting for you.

This is your time.

Oh! All the names I've used as examples were changed and many stories were slightly modified.

# Step 1:

# Self-Assessment - The Foundation of a Successful Career Transition

Before you embark on a journey to a new career, it's vital to understand yourself thoroughly. Self-assessment involves deep introspection and analysis, enabling you to make informed decisions about your future path. This process goes far beyond the traditional "know thyself" concept, delving into various critical aspects:

### A. Values and Passions: Unearthing Your Driving Forces

Our core values and passions act as an internal compass, guiding us toward meaningful work that energizes rather than depletes us. When our career aligns with these fundamental tenets, we experience a profound sense of purpose and fulfillment.

But how do you pinpoint your true values and obsessions? It requires honest self-reflection. What issues or causes ignite a fire within you? What activities leave you feeling gratified and centered? Make a list and see what themes emerge.

For some, it may be a passion for creativity and self-expression through art, writing, or design. Others are driven by a desire to help others, whether through healthcare, teaching, or social services. And many are motivated by income potential or entrepreneurial freedom.

I've seen transformations when people get in touch with their deepest values. Sarah was unfulfilled in marketing until volunteering at a conservation center rekindled her childhood love of nature. "It was like something clicked into place," she told me. "Protecting the environment - that's my true calling." This passion drove her transition into renewable energy.

Another person, James, realized his work-life balance and autonomy were non-negotiables after the birth of his first child. His former role's long hours and rigid policies conflicted with his values of being a present father and maintaining control over his schedule. This clarity empowered him to launch a consulting business from home.

On the other hand, money was the prime motivator for Jane, a single mother determined to break the poverty cycle for her children. Her list of non-negotiable values included financial security, providing educational opportunities, and leaving a legacy. This focused her job search on higher-paying fields like finance and technology.

Your values may encompass creativity, independence, structure, intellectual growth, social impact - the list is endless. Perhaps you're passionate about a specific subject like history, animal welfare, or music. Get granular about what matters most.

Once you unmask these core tenets, you open the door to career paths that will be sustaining rather than draining. You can prioritize roles aligned with your obsessions and authentic sense of purpose. The result is deeply rewarding work that lets you honor your values each day.

## B. Skills and Talents: Unlocking Your Marketable Assets

When considering a career transition, your skills and talents are valuable assets to leverage. These are the tools in your arsenal that can transfer across industries and roles. By taking inventory of what you naturally excel at and what abilities you've honed over time, you empower yourself to explore opportunities that may not be immediately obvious.

Start by making a comprehensive list of every skill you possess - no matter how big or small. Include hard skills like coding, data analysis, and project management, as well as soft skills like communication, emotional intelligence, and creative thinking. Don't overthink it - just do a brain dump initially and get it all out on paper.

Next, assess which skills come most naturally to you. Maybe you're a gifted writer who is able to express complex ideas in easy-to-understand ways. Or you have an intuitive way of connecting with people and reading between the emotional lines. These innate skills are powerful differentiators.

Then look at skills you've diligently developed through experience and training, like proficiency in software programs, languages, or specialties within your current field. My client Miguel was a self-taught WordPress expert from tinkering with websites as a marketing manager. This allowed him to pivot into a web developer role.

It's also important to identify areas where you have potential but need further training or education. Perhaps you have natural creativity but lack formal design skills. Note those growth opportunities as well.

Reframing how you view your skills is key. Sarah was stuck in an accounting rut until I reexamined her talents through a new lens. Her exceptional organizational abilities, eye for detail, and analytical skills were incredibly transferable - making her a perfect fit for a project manager role that allowed her to build the systems she craved.

Don't be afraid to think in atypical ways and connect seemingly unrelated skills. I had a client who was a former ballet dancer - an incredible asset for her current career as an agile coach, where she accelerated team coordination through skills like spatial awareness and choreography.

The most marketable professionals are constantly adding to their skill repertoires. Seek out courses, certifications, or experiences (like volunteering) that allow you to acquire new abilities aligned with your passion. Continuous learning is essential in our rapidly evolving workforce. By comprehensively evaluating your skills - both innate and learned - you will uncover exciting opportunities that may have been previously inaccessible or off your radar. It will open up a new world of possibilities for that elusive career fit.

## C. Interests and Hobbies: Where Passion Meets Profession

Too often, we compartmentalize work as something separate from what fulfills us personally. But our hobbies and interests are windows into the activities that truly light us up inside. When we connect these passions with our professional pursuits, we unlock intensely rewarding career opportunities.

I've witnessed incredible transformations when clients realize their leisure activities could evolve into dream jobs. Mike was trapped in the finance world, feeling numb and uninspired for years. But woodworking was his oasis - a beloved hobby since childhood. As we explored this further, he waxed poetic about lovingly running his hands along different woods, the satisfaction of crafting something from scratch, combining form with function.

It was a lightbulb moment. Mike's creative energy and attention to detail were tailor-made for a career as a furniture designer and maker. He went back to school for industrial design, started selling custom pieces on the side, and within a few years launched a high-end furniture brand. The pure joy on his face now is a stark contrast to his former burned-out banker self. For Sasha, a self-professed "hobby-collector," her love of baking was what ultimately revealed her true calling. From the precise science of ratios to the artistic expression of decorating, she was hooked. Sasha started a baking blog during her corporate job, connecting with enthusiasts globally and hosting virtual baking classes on the side. When she was let go during the pandemic, she seized on it as a chance to pursue her passion full-time by opening her own baking studio and school.

Sometimes interests reveal crucial skills that can transfer directly. An avid gamer like Lucas has potential in roles like UX design, leveraging skills in interface development, and creating engaging experiences. Or the organized sports team captain who excels at motivation and strategy could transition to a project management career in time.

Even simple hobbies have value - a love of travel could evolve into a remote role, event planning could mean a career in hospitality, and interest in fashion could open the door to roles in ecommerce or buying. Essentially, any activity that gets you "in flow" and lights up your passion is worth exploring professionally.

Making this mind shift - valuing hobbies as more than casual pastimes - allows you to reimagine work as something energizing rather than dreaded. It permits you to intertwine what you love with what you do. And that's the ultimate recipe for a fulfilling career.

## D. Personality and Work Style: The Path to Productive Passion

We all have distinct personality traits and work styles that influence the environments where we thrive. Identifying yours is key to aligning your career with an atmosphere that amplifies your strengths rather than drains your energy reserves.

Some people are invigorated by interpersonal collaboration and client-facing roles, while others prefer more independence and behind-the-scenes contributions. There's no universal "best" work style, which is why self-awareness is crucial.

Emma was an extroverted "people-person" stuck in a solitary clerical role. Her bubbly personality and ability to build rapport were stifled by the isolating nature of her work. Helping her transition into a client success role where she could regularly interact with customers was a game-changer. "I finally had an outlet for my natural chattiness!" she said with a radiant smile.

On the flip side, Noah was an introvert who dreaded the group dynamics and constant social interactions of his consulting job. His sweet spot was independent research and analysis. Helping him pivot into a behind-the-scenes business intelligence role gave him the autonomy he craved to dive deep into analytics without interruption.

Work style preferences around structure and flexibility are also critical factors. Some thrive with clearly defined processes, expectations, and hierarchies. Others need more creative freedom and flexibility in their days. When someone's needs clash with the environment, it breeds frustration.

Take Janelle, an entrepreneur at heart who always struggled in corporate bureaucracies with excessive red tape and rigid policies. Helping her launch a PR consulting firm allowed her natural self-motivation and abstract thinking style to shine. In contrast, Sarah, a military veteran, felt rudderless without more clearly defined systems and leadership until she found an operations role with an established chain of command.

Work-life balance and scheduling needs are also part of this equation. The ability to work remotely or weird hours could be a top priority for some, while others need the structure and socialization of being in an office.

There are personality tests like Myers-Briggs that can provide insight, but I also rely on deep discussions to understand a client's core needs. What situations drain or energize them? When do they feel most productive and creative? How do they best take in information?

The most rewarding careers are those that feel tailored to your own operating system rather than requiring you to constantly override your own natural code. By getting clear on your personality and ideal environment, you can explore roles that feel less like an ill-fitting uniform and more like a freeing expression of your true self.

There are many test you can take that will offer ideas. These tests will indicate personality attributes that would make you a good fit for this kind of work.

The first one is 123 Career Test. It's a simple, easy-to-use career aptitude test that identifies careers that might make a match for your personality. You will take a yes-no answer based on preferences for different pictures that you see. That's pretty easy.

The second one is the O*NET Interest Profiler, which the US Government Department of Labor supports. It will make suggestions based on interest tendencies.

The third one is the Keirsey Temperament Sorter. It helps identify your temperament within a work environment and your personality type. Based on the results, it labels your personality as either a guardian, artisan, rational or idealist, and provides you with a description of your temperament and personality profile with the option to pay for a complete report.

The fourth is the Princeton Review Career Quiz. This aptitude test offers career suggestions based on your style and interests as they relate to the workplace. 24 questions help them figure this out.

Fifth is TestColor. Complete a two-part selection process in which you choose various colors. Based upon the colors you select, the test gives you an initial analysis of your personality and career aptitude. They will try to upsell you for a more in-depth analysis of the results and further career.

Sixth is PathSource, an app for mobile that provides you with career options based on your personality and interests. It provides an extensive database of jobs based on academic achievements, such as different types of degrees.

Eight is the MAPP career test. That stands for Motivational Appraisal of Personal Potential career test. It's an assessment that provides career suggestions, again, based on your personality, and helps you determine what your career motivations are, and the top vocational categories in which you're most likely to excel.

## E. Life Goals: Crafting a Career Congruent With Your Vision

Careers don't exist in a vacuum - they are inextricably linked to the grander aspirations we have for our lives. Taking time to reflect on your bigger life goals ensures that the career you pursue acts as a stepping stone rather than a detour on your journey.

Start by envisioning where you'd like to be in 5, 10, or even 20 years from now. What does your best life look like? The size of your family, where you live, what lifestyle you want , impact you make? Get granular about your hopes and dreams for the future.

For some, their career may serve as the primary vehicle for achieving certain life goals. Samantha wanted to build a profitable business she could pass down to her children one day, leaving a legacy. This motivated her to transition into entrepreneurship by opening a marketing agency.

For others, a career is more of a means to fund their actual life aspirations.

Jack's main goal was to have the flexibility to spend summers traveling across Europe with his family. He sought out a career where people commonly work remotely that would give him that freedom each year.

Consider whether you prioritize work-life balance and having ample free time versus climbing a corporate ladder focused more singularly on career achievements. Maybe your goal is to accumulate enough wealth to retire early and pursue passion projects guilt-free.

Perhaps you are someone with social impact goals that a career path could help or hinder. Lisa sought out roles at mission-driven nonprofits and B-Corps after having her first child sparked a desire to leave a positive imprint on the world her daughter would inherit.

Don't forget to factor in personal values like financial security, work-life integration, autonomy, intellectual growth, or global experience. These could shape the types of industries and roles you target.

I've had clients realize their full-time jobs were detracting from bigger life goals like writing a book, running a farm, or spending more time with family. That reframing prompted career pivots more conducive to those objectives.

By reverse-engineering from your ideal future vision, you can select a career trajectory that actively supports those aims, rather than leaving you feeling you sacrificed your dreams for a paycheck. It's the best way to achieve holistic, lasting life satisfaction in the decades ahead.

## F. Feedback from Others: Unlocking An Outside-In View

We often lack objectivity about our talents and abilities. The skills or qualities we take for granted as "no big deal" may be what makes us truly exceptional in the eyes of others. That's why seeking an outside perspective from those who know you best can be so insightful during a career transition.

My client, Sarah, was considering leaving her corporate marketing role but felt paralyzed about what path to take next. While she loved writing, she didn't see it as a viable career option. That's when her husband chimed in: "Are you kidding? You're an incredible writer! Everything you put together is engaging and connects with people on an emotional level."

His affirmation gave Sarah the nudge of confidence she needed. She began freelance writing on the side, gaining experience and exposure. Within a year, she had built up enough client work to resign from her marketing job and launch her own copywriting business full-time.

Sometimes it's our closest friends and family members who can pinpoint our hidden strengths. Justin always brushed off his ability to explain complex technical concepts in simple terms. To him, it felt second nature. But his college buddies marveled at how he could take something they struggled to grasp and break it down in a relatable, easy-to-understand way.

Recognizing this gift for taking the complex and making it accessible opened up a path for Justin as a technical trainer and curriculum developer - careers he had never considered.

Former colleagues and managers can also shed light on talents that may have gone unnoticed or undervalued. Maybe you collaborated cross-functionally more effectively than your peers. Or you excelled at managing up and communicating with leadership in a clear, confident style.

I'll never forget what a former boss told my client Claire: "You have this incredible ability to look at all sides of an issue and pinpoint the root cause, even when it's not obvious. You just intuitively make connections that others miss." Coming from her manager reframed Claire's critical thinking skills as better suited for a role in strategic consulting than her current marketing gig.

Don't discount positive feedback that seems insignificant. When compiling input, look for patterns and themes. If multiple people highlight the same strength, it's worth considering how that talent could fuel your next career move.

An outside vantage point is invaluable for gaining perspective on what makes you unique and marketable. Oftentimes, just hearing an objective voice reaffirm, "You're really good at X," can be the push we need to confidently pursue new opportunities that maximize our potential.

## G. Cultural and Ethical Considerations: Honoring Your Values

Our career choices shouldn't exist in a moral vacuum. The professional environments we opt into have a major impact on our wellbeing and sense of fulfillment. That's why it's critical to reflect on your cultural and ethical values during this self-assessment process.

For some, prioritizing certain cultural elements like diversity, equity, and inclusion initiatives is non-negotiable. My client Jamal shared how alienating it felt to be one of the only people of color at his former company. Even small things like inconsistent enforcement of the dress code rubbed him the wrong way. He knew his next role needed to be with an organization that genuinely embraced multiculturalism.

I helped Jamal identify companies that were highly rated for DEI and had actively anti-racist cultures and practices. His face lit up when describing the inclusive vibe during interviews at his current workplace, which has a chief diversity officer and employee resource groups.

For others, ethical and moral considerations take precedence. Arya, who follows a vegan lifestyle, felt immense inner conflict working for a pharmaceutical company that conducted animal testing. Despite her passion for science, she felt compelled to adhere to her beliefs by finding employment in an industry like biotech or plant-based nutrition that aligned with her ethics.

Then there was Liam, who walked away from a high-paying consulting role because he couldn't stomach committing to perpetuating systems he saw as ecologically destructive. We had to get creative about pivoting him into more sustainable fields like renewable energy and environmental protection.

Sometimes the cultural or ethical issues are more subtle but still crucial deal-breakers. Tanya, who emigrated from Southeast Asia, placed a high premium on finding an organization that respected and accommodated her need to observe certain religious holidays. During interviews, she made a point to ask about faith-based policies.

Even corporate social responsibility practices could be an ethical litmus test. One client felt strongly about only working for B-Corps or companies that meet green business standards and have robust sustainability commitments.

It's too easy to make compromises when you're eager to leave an unfulfilling job. But ensuring your core values aren't violated in your next role is essential for long-term happiness and success. I always encourage people to audit potential employers through resources like employee review sites and by asking thoughtful questions throughout the interview process.

Your career path should enrich your life, not leave you battling moral dilemmas or cultural discord daily. Prioritizing these factors allows you to pinpoint organizations and roles that are a holistic match for who you are.

## H. Challenges and Fears: Confronting What Holds You Back

While an exciting career transition holds so much possibility, it's also fraught with potential roadblocks that can sabotage your success if left unaddressed. Being honest about your fears and perceived challenges is crucial for overcoming them.

For many, financial uncertainties loom the largest. How will you sustain yourself through a potential pay cut or time off for additional education? My client Mark fretted about supporting his family when he shared his dream of becoming a teacher after over a decade in sales. We mapped out a transition budget and looked at ways his wife could temporarily increase her hours. Putting a plan in place helped quell his fears.

Then there are the psychological hurdles - the doubts that you're too old to make a major change or the imposter syndrome of feeling unqualified for a new field. Anna, a 40-something executive assistant felt paralyzed about pivoting into her passion-- graphic design. "The industry is flooded with younger creatives. How can I possibly compete?" Defining her strengths, building up a portfolio through volunteering, and connecting with supportive design mentors ultimately gave her the confidence boost needed to launch her firm.

Concerns about investing precious time and money into retraining and education can also breed hesitation. For Jose, an immigrant parent supporting his family overseas, sinking his life savings into a data science bootcamp felt like a massive gamble. Outlining a stepwise plan where he could start taking online classes while working helped ease his mind.

Then there are the clients whose biggest hurdles are more personal - whether it's overcoming self-doubt, analysis paralysis, or a crippling fear of failure instilled by well-meaning but misguided loved ones. "What if I end up hating this new career too?" they may wonder. Unpacking those reservations through journaling, talk therapy, or life coaching can be transformative.

I also guide people through developing contingency plans to address potential setbacks, like having a "Side Hustle Sabbatical" where they can test-drive a new field before diving in fully. Or taking things one step at a time through incremental career experimentation before making the full leap.

Whenever fears or doubts arise, I have people get specific about naming them - writing them down verbatim. It's remarkable how simply giving anxieties a label and voice can dilute their power. From there, we can strategize ways to neutralize them through tactics like positive mantras, building supportive networks, and celebrating small wins along the way.
While the path ahead may feel daunting at times, avoiding your fears often leads to a far scarier fate - awakening years down the road to the regret of a dream deferred. Staring them down today can safeguard your future from that remorse. An honest reckoning with your reservations clears the road for an inspiring journey.

Perhaps one of the most empowering realizations in life is that you never truly "arrive" at a fixed, finalized version of yourself. We are constantly evolving beings. The "Self" is more of a working theory than an immutable fact carved in stone. This means your self-assessment for a career transition must be viewed as an ever-unfolding journey of deepening self-discovery, not just a single evaluation.

Think back to who you were 5 or 10 years ago. Your priorities, interests, strengths - so much has likely shifted and expanded since then. You contain multitudes, each layer becoming unearthed gradually like an archeological excavation. The self-assessment process simply dusts off the uppermost strata, giving hints at what lies beneath. But to fully explore your depths and uncover your most authentic, satisfied self, you must keep digging.

That's why practices like journaling, where you can grapple with existential questions and observe your innermost thoughts, are so powerful. Getting your subconscious reflections out of your head and onto paper or a\the technology of your choosing provides an objective surface for making sense of your amorphous feelings and identities. You may be surprised by the revelations that emerge - creative sparks you'd dampened, entrepreneurial fires you'd unconsciously smothered, or passions that reignite when revisited.

Meditation serves a similar purpose. Using intentional stillness to let your mind slowly settle so you can see through to the clearest waters of your core self. When we're constantly bombarded by external noise and distractions, we lose touch with our innate guiding voices. But sitting for just 10-20 minutes daily can be enough to restore that intuitive clarity.

Of course, working one-on-one with a career coach provides structured guidance for this infinite self-exploration. Think of it like being handed a metal detector and map for your unique inner terrain. A skilled coach can sense where to dig based on your proclivities, challenge you to push beyond self-limiting beliefs, and ensure you're comprehensively surveying every dimension of your psyche. They're part facilitator, part anthropologist, helping you excavate and examine your intrinsic drives.

The deeper you go into understanding your true self, the more capable you'll become at finding a career that's soul-satisfying rather than soul-sucking. Each new role then becomes another enlightening voyage of learning more about who you are and what you're meant to contribute to this world. It's a perpetual, fascinating cycle of thrilling and frightening self-rediscovery.

# Step 2:

# Define Your Goals and Let Them Guide You

In any major life transition, having a clear set of guiding goals is essential. They act as your compass, map, and North Star all in one. Without well-defined objectives, you risk aimlessly wandering through the wilderness of career change, expending precious energy without direction. But with purposefully plotted goals, each step becomes intentional progress toward your desired destination.

Start by getting radically honest with yourself about what a successful career transition looks like to you. Is it landing a role with a specific job title, salary level, company, or industry? Or are your aims more aligned with achieving certain lifestyle benchmarks like more flexibility, work-life balance, or geographical preferences? Perhaps your goals involve developing new skills, finding more meaning, or reaching an income threshold that allows you to pursue other passions.

Whatever your vision of the promised land, ensure your transition goals are as specific and measurable as possible. "Finding a more fulfilling job" is too abstract to be actionable. "Securing a remote marketing manager role with a mission-driven B-Corp that pays between $80k-$100k" provides far clearer mile markers to orient yourself.

It's also smart to set a mix of shorter and longer-term objectives to track along the way. Completing a social media marketing certification could be a near-term goal that builds towards the bigger aim of landing that remote marketing role. This staggered approach allows you to chunk an intimidating transition into more palatable steps while still visually reaching regular micro-victories.

Be cautious about accidentally diminishing your own goals out of self-doubt or external pressures. So many clients arrive with lofty yet unvoiced desires that get mistakenly watered down to more "realistic" aims based on what others think is attainable. But you're the architect of this voyage - don't be afraid to dream boldly and design the career you truly want.

With your customized career transition goals mapped out, suddenly the path toward fulfilling work starts coming into focused clarity. You'll know what actions and strategies will propel you closer...and which detours to avoid entirely. Murky uncertainty gets replaced by an empowering sense of agency. Those goals become a motivational mantra reminding you of the "why" behind the blood, sweat, and tears.

So don't let the fear of getting lost deter you from making a needed career pivot. Create your own tailored transition goals and use them as a reliable guidepost to navigate this exciting next chapter. With clearly defined objectives as your lodestar, you'll always know exactly which direction will take you closer to the fulfillment you seek.

## Clarity is Key

Start by getting clear on exactly what you hope to achieve in this career pivot. Ambiguity will only breed confusion and inertia. Drill down into the specific details, considering:

**Job/Role:** What is the precise position or job title you're aiming for? Don't settle for vague terms like "something creative." Get granular - graphic designer, UX writer, art director?

**Industry/Sector:** Which particular industry is the best ecosystem for your target role? Tech, advertising, publishing, etc? Vet out the spaces where you'll thrive.

**Location:** Where is your geographic bullseye for employment? A specific city, or state, or are you open to remote work from anywhere? Factor in cost of living.

Salary & Benefits: What is your absolute minimum compensation threshold to make this transition viable? Benefits like health insurance, 401k, etc are also crucial.

**Work-Life Balance:** Do you want a strict 9-5? Flexible or remote hours? Will this career enable your ideal integrated lifestyle?

The more explicit you can be upfront about exactly what "success" looks like, the easier it becomes to reverse engineer the roadmap to get there.

## Short-Term & Long-Term Goals

It's also wise to distinguish between shorter-term goals that act as stepping stones versus your bigger, long-range vision. This helps chunk an intimidating transition into manageable, motivating milestones.

For example, your short-term goals may include acquiring certain skills, credentials or experience over the next 6-12 months. While your long-term goals could be about reaching particular income levels or leadership roles 3-5 years out.

Maybe your short-term aim is completing a data analytics bootcamp and doing an internship, paving the way for your long-term goal of becoming a data scientist at a major tech firm. Having these segmented checkpoints provides clear pathways to measure progress.

## Measurable Goals

This brings us to quantifying your objectives to make them tangible and measurable. Vague aspirations like "get a better job" are impossible to track.

Instead, attach concrete numbers, dates, or skills to your targets. "Land a Product Manager role with a base salary between $90k-110k within 9 months" gives you something palpable to aim for and evaluate your advancement towards.

This quantification is crucial for both bolstering your commitment and evaluating your strategies. If you're not closing in on measurable goals according to the timeline you've defined, it's a signal to adjust your transition plan.

## Realistic & Achievable

Now for a quick dose of reality - As motivating as it can feel to shoot for the moon, anchor at least some of your goals in what's pragmatic and achievable based on your current qualifications and circumstances.

We don't want to completely curb your ambition and aim low, but balance is key so you don't get derailed by discouragement from constantly falling short of pie-in-the-sky expectations.

Look at the typical paths and requirements for your target career, then set goals that show a logical progression based on your existing skills and experience. Perhaps start with job titles one step below your ultimate destination as you build applicable skills.

You can always modify and elevate goals that prove too easy to attain. But having some realistic "quick wins" helps build confidence and sustain momentum.

## Alignment with Values

Throughout this goal-setting process, keep referring back to your core values identified in your self-assessment work. Your career transition goals should feel congruent with what matters most to you philosophically.

If one of your driving values is work-life balance to be more present with family, yet your objectives are leading you towards a notoriously overworked career path, you're headed for a values conflict. Realign those goals to restore integrity.

This intersection of goals and values is essential for achieving true fulfillment. Don't let the destination sacrifice your sense of self and purpose.

## Timeframes

The final critical component is assigning clear timeframes to your goals to instill urgency and momentum. Open-ended desires tend to get deprioritized. But declaring you'll acquire a certain certification by Q3 or launch your freelance side gig by the new year creates structured accountability.

# Step 3:

# Networking: Forge Connections

For too long, networking has gotten a bad rap as something transactional - simply amassing LinkedIn connections or business cards as some checkbox to be hit. But in the context of a career transition, it is absolutely essential to develop an authentic network. These relationships can elevate you into a new professional stratosphere.

At its core, effective networking is about cultivating meaningful, mutually beneficial connections with others who can provide insights, guidance, exposure, ideas, and opportunities you may not otherwise have access to. After all, it's valuable to have trusted allies in your corner who've traveled the path you're venturing down and can illuminate potential pitfalls. It's also valuable to know connectors who can facilitate warm introductions to decision-makers in your target industry.

Forging these bonds takes genuine effort and emotional investment beyond just dutifully attending stilted mixer events. You have to bring curiosity, vulnerability, generosity of spirit, and patience to the process. It's about discovering how you can support one another's goals in a symbiotic way over the long haul while developing trust.

One of my favorite examples is my client Mark, an aspiring entrepreneur seeking to launch an apparel brand focused on sustainable materials. While networking, he developed a friendship with a fashion merchandiser named Wandy who had a wealth of supply chain knowledge. In exchange for Mark's savvy social media advice to elevate her profile, Wandy became an invaluable mentor introducing him to ethical suppliers and manufacturers to explore partnerships.

By leading with a spirit of generosity first, Mark cultivated an incredibly valuable relationship on a foundation of trust rather than just a self-serving transactional ask. These are the types of resonant connections that ultimately usher you into new professional circles.

Approaching networking with that level of authenticity - seeking to genuinely add value to others while organically exploring mutual areas of synergy - is key. From establishing role models and mentors to gain advice and exposure, to seeding relationships with potential partners, clients, or employers down the line, investing in your network is akin to planting seeds you can nurture for an eventual career bloom.But of course, strategic effort and focus are still required to reap maximum growth.

## Define Your Networking Goals

Having a clear "why" behind your networking approach is crucial for prioritizing your efforts and interactions. Aimlessly accumulating contacts without purpose can quickly lead to scattershot energy and a lack of meaningful traction.

Get granular about what exactly you hope to gain through cultivating new connections during this career transition. Potential objectives could include:

Advice & Mentorship: Perhaps your primary aim is to build relationships with seasoned professionals in your target field who can coach you through common pitfalls and unwritten rules. Jessica was pivoting from marketing to UX design. Her top goal was finding UX mentors who could advise her on prioritizing which skills to develop, how to showcase a portfolio and insights about company cultures that truly value user experience.

Job Leads & Introductions: For some, networking is a means of unearthing unadvertised job opportunities and facilitating warm handoffs to new companies. David leveraged his existing network to set up informational interviews at firms in his desired cyber-security sphere. This enabled him to get his foot in the door for potential openings while also vetting the organization's culture.

Industry Expertise & Trends: Staying ahead of the curve on shifting industry landscapes and future priorities is invaluable when changing careers.

Milan, an educator, established networking goals around connecting with learning & development leaders across different sectors. This helped her gain a macro view of which pedagogical methodologies and modalities were gaining traction to ensure her skills stayed aligned with market needs.

Support System: Don't underestimate the value of simply making new friends and having an empathetic support system cheering you on through the stressful upheaval of changing careers. This acted as Ryan's primary networking focus after going through a divorce - he prioritized connecting with other solopreneurs who could relate to his unique lifestyle transitional challenges.

Once you get clear on your overarching goals, you can then strategically identify which types of events, communities, people, and platforms make sense to invest time into versus allowing yourself to get distracted. Having an explicit "why" keeps you focused on nurturing contacts with maximum relevance and value.

**Leverage Your Existing Network**

While it's smart to proactively build new connections, don't overlook the powerful potential within your existing network of relationships. Those you already know - whether friends, family, former colleagues or acquaintances - can open doors you may have overlooked.

Samantha made the mistake of assuming her social circle couldn't help her pivot into data science since none worked in tech. Big mistake! Once she clarified her goals, former coworkers rallied around her. Joan, who worked in marketing, connected her with a neighbor - a data scientist willing to be an informal mentor. Samantha's college buddy Tom helped land her first data science internship by giving a glowing referral to his boss.

The truth is, your network is more robust and resourceful than you think if you make the effort to enlist their support. But it requires being transparent about your transition plans and giving them clear avenues to get involved beyond vague well-wishes.

Michael shared his aspirations of becoming a high school counselor during his kid's PTA meeting. A few weeks later, he received a casual email from a parent he barely knew - the principal at a nearby school offering to put him in touch with their college counseling department for potential shadowing opportunities. This warm introduction fostered by existing community ties helped Michael get a foot in the door to start gaining critical experience.

Friends can often connect you to "friends of friends" creating indirect links to valuable new contacts. Megan, who wanted to launch her own PR firm, leveraged her inner circle to get introductions to marketing leaders at major brands who became a few of her first clients. The key is arming your existing connections with the right verbiage to endorse your background and skillsets.

Don't make assumptions about who may (or may not) be able to help with your transition. Often, it's loose social ties that end up being most impactful - like former coworkers from unrelated industries or even college acquaintances you haven't spoken to in years. Greg was shocked when his fraternity brother's new girlfriend, upon hearing about his medical coding interest, introduced him to her hospital CEO father who gave him a crash course in the field.

The best networks are permeable webs continuously expanding and evolving. It starts with respectfully rallying and reintroducing your closest contacts to your latest professional evolution with thoughtful context. Those already in your circle often hold net-expanding capabilities if you simply make the ask.

## Online Networking: Forging Digital Inroads

In a hyper-connected world like ours, your networking efforts aren't limited to in-person events and face-to-face interactions. The digital landscape provides ample opportunities to create new connections and immerse yourself in online communities for your target industry.

LinkedIn has become an indispensable tool for expanding your network and increasing visibility during a career pivot. But simply having a profile isn't enough - you need to optimize your personal brand and leverage LinkedIn's features intentionally.

Mark carefully reframed his LinkedIn headline and "About" section to position himself as a passionate newcomer to the renewable energy space, eagerly seeking mentorship opportunities. This set the tone and allowed him to naturally initiate conversations with credible green tech leaders he hoped to learn from.

Joining industry-relevant LinkedIn or Facebook groups can also open doors. Sarah, a former teacher exploring instructional design roles, actively participated in discussions within an eLearning group. She offered insights from her classroom experiences while picking up on emerging trends and tech tools. This raised her credibility and led to informational interviews with members who were impressed by her curiosity.

Facebook and Instagram provide avenues for tracking companies you're interested in as well. By following brands and engaging with their social media content, you can stay updated on new initiatives, products, personnel changes as well as potential job openings. Several clients have landed interviews simply by being the first to spot and apply to newly advertised roles shared in a company's Instagram story.

Online platforms democratize access in ways unheard of before the internet. With some strategic positioning and consistent nurturing, you can virtually "meet" and build relationships with gatekeepers and influencers who were previously untouchable.

Of course, the inherent risk is letting online interactions become a crutch, substituting weak ties for deeper relationship building. The best networking combines the outreach capabilities of digital platforms with intentional human connection. Use the online realm to identify and initiate promising contacts, but seal the deal by taking it offline as quickly as possible.

From introductions facilitated via a LinkedIn inMail to spontaneous X DM conversations that reveal synergies, there's immense networking power available. Make sure you upgrade these connections to make them more valuable.

## Attend Industry Events: Immerse Yourself in the Ecosystem

While online networking casts a wide net, there's no substitute for the power of face-to-face connections formed by immersing yourself in physical events and meetups populating your new professional community. This is where you can develop rapport rapidly and obtain priceless insider access. Conferences and trade shows provide a chance to mix with key players, thought leaders and trailblazers driving your target industry forward. Arianna was able to interact with her marketing professionals and a few of her heroes by attending a few strategically chosen annual conventions. This elevated her from an anonymous aspiring creative to an increasingly recognized figure.

The networking opportunities extend far beyond just the main panels and sessions. Some of the most valuable relationship-building happens at the ancillary social gatherings, receptions, and after-parties where you can connect with professionals in lower-stakes environments. Arianna landed her new career and job after hitting it off with a Creative Director over drinks at the hotel bar following a conference.

While mulling a career 180 into real estate investment, Eric made it a point to regularly attend local property investor association meetings. These relatively casual meetups allowed him to observe and learn about the very deals, properties, and partnerships that excited him most. He was able to candidly ask questions and receive mentorship from seasoned investors happy to share their experiences with an eager newcomer showing genuine interest.

Don't restrict yourself solely to the largest or most prestigious events either. Some of the most invigorating communities can be found at niche local and regional meetup groups. When Naomi sought to transition from nursing into health & wellness coaching, she discovered a thriving ecosystem by attending intimate workshops and masterminds hosted by influential practitioners in her area. The vulnerability and collaboration she witnessed at these smaller gatherings ultimately inspired her in her new career.

Webinars can be a great introductory first step for getting exposure to your intended new field from the comfort of your current lifestyle too. Many events offer virtual tickets to allow you to get a taste of the insights, lingo, and key players before investing in pricier travel or in-person commitments.

The key is to be extremely intentional about your event investments of time and money. Do your research to uncover the most relevant and enriching opportunities that will maximize your ability to forge new connections and facilitate your successful career transition. Have a strategy for the key people you hope to meet and relationships you aim to initiate. Making random appearances as a wallflower won't do - you have to be willing to be visible, engaged, and assertive.

Events are temporary worlds where you get to embody your future reality in ways difficult to replicate elsewhere. Leveraging them purposefully can help rapidly accelerate your aspirational trajectory from outsider to industry insider.

## Informational Interviews: Gaining the Insider's Perspective

Increasingly, forward-thinking professionals are turning to informational interviews as one of the most powerful tools in their career transition arsenal. These casual meetings, distinct from job interviews, provide an intimate glimpse into a new field from the ultimate source - those already working within it.

At its core, an informational interview is respectfully requesting to pick someone's brain in exchange for a free coffee, lunch, or simply their time. The agenda is driven by your curiosities about their roles, day-to-day experiences, insights into emerging trends, career journey stories, and whatever else you're eager to understand and them to share.

Miguel was apprehensive about leaving his financial analyst role for the uncertainty of UX design. A few informational interviews helped demystify his concerns. Meeting with UXers at both startups and large companies illuminated the variety of potential paths and environments. Soon, he felt reassured this new field aligned with his mentality and creative strengths.

For Sara, these meetings provided a window into company cultures notoriously tricky to assess from the outside. As an HR manager exploring opportunities in tech, speaking with insiders across different firms helped her discern which types of organizations and leadership teams truly prioritized work-life balance and psychological safety - her top criteria.

Beyond ensuring the right personal fit, informational interviews shed light on the unwritten rules and political dynamics of an industry. Lee leveraged this access while plotting his transition into real estate private equity. Speaking with acquisition managers clued him into subtle yet critical nuances around how developers, investors, and city officials interact behind closed doors versus textbook theories.

Naturally, these meetings are also prime relationship-building opportunities. Trisha formed a lasting mentor connection by expressing her genuine enthusiasm and intellectual curiosity to a senior marketing executive she admired during their talk. That rapport helped Trisha land an entry-level role at the same company months later and a relationship with a trusted adviser for years to come.

While in-person interviews are ideal, virtual meetings have become increasingly embraced for convenience. Anita seamlessly conducted video interviews with nurses across different specializations and geographies as she re-imagined her path after burning out from the pandemic. She adeptly leveraged recording features to revisit nuggets of insight at her leisure during the decision process.

At their core, informational interviews are like receiving an amazing college guest lecture for free. Approach them with the mindset of being an eager learner and soak up as much as you can. Be sure to reciprocate generously by expressing gratitude afterward and finding ways to add value back to your interviewer's work or life.

There are few instances where you'll gain such unprecedented access into the realities of a new field and the psyche of its people. Informational interviews, leveraged consistently and authentically, are precious career transition opportunities not to be squandered.

## Professional Associations: A Target Rich Zone for Connections

While conferences and meetups are extraordinary for initial exposure, few institutions provide as comprehensive an insider's view into a new industry quite like professional associations. These member organizations are often where real movers, shakers, and subject matter experts convene to swap best practices and shape their professional realms.

By joining the ranks of a respected association relevant to your desired field, you're effectively purchasing a VIP pass to plug into that world's central nervous system. From tailored training programs and certification opportunities to special interest groups diving into hyper-niche topics, these communities highlight insights and emerging trends that could otherwise take years to intuit from the outside.

When Samantha decided to pivot into user experience design after a decade in marketing, joining a user experience group accelerated her transition. Suddenly, she had access to localized meetups, virtual workshops, research libraries, and job boards tailored explicitly for UX practitioners. These resources helped quickly upskill her while expanding her network of potential mentors and hiring managers.

Similarly, Jonathan was able to immerse himself in the accounting ecosystem by joining the American Institute of Certified Public Accountants (AICPA) and state-based affiliates. Book studies, leadership conferences, and peer-to-peer discussion forums helped him to stay abreast of new regulations, tools, and perspectives on issues like tax compliance, financial reporting, and practice optimization. This knowledge deepened his credibility for landing accounting roles despite coming from an adjacent corporate finance background.

The benefits of professional memberships often extend far beyond the explicitly defined. For entrepreneurs and freelancers, joining an association introduces you to your ideal clients or customer base. Marissa started attending local chapter meetings of one while freelancing to elevate her visibility with companies seeking contract marketing support. Several clients ended up hiring her after seeing her exhibit leadership and innovative thinking in association workshops.

Many associations provide channels for attaining accredited certifications and credentials that can enhance your marketability. Bill enrolled in the Project Management Institute (PMI) to start working towards his PMP certification, ensuring his IT management skills translated when pivoting into a product leadership role. The PMI's local meetings also allowed him to recruit potential team members for future projects.

Perhaps most importantly, professional associations facilitate connections with inspirational mentors who can light paths you may not envision otherwise. Allison joined the American Counseling Association (ACA) and its subgroups focused explicitly on her clinical interests. There, she met seasoned experts willing to coach an eager student eager to transcend traditional modalities. Those mentorships revealed transformative new approaches she's since taken her counseling practice in exciting new directions.

While annual fees can add up, reputable associations offer invaluable knowledge, community, and foresight to avoid amateur pitfalls when entering new career terrain. By paying your dues to join these inner circles, you're investing in your long-term ability to not just participate in your new field, but help mold and elevate it for years to come.

## Volunteer and Community Engagement: Experimenting with the Change

For many, a career change is fueled by a desire to align their work with societal impact and deeper meaning. If that resonates, then volunteering or engaging with mission-driven community projects provides the perfect complement to your networking efforts. It allows you to prove your convictions while building critical relationships and skills, while experimenting in a new field without having to make a total break from your current work so quickly.

Maria felt disconnected from her corporate finance role despite the lucrative paycheck. What reinvigorated her was volunteering as a money coach for low-income families through a local nonprofit. Witnessing the tangible impact of empowering others with financial literacy rekindled

Maria's sense of purpose. It also exposed her to mentors and collaborators in the personal finance ecosystem she hopes to transition towards.

This type of skilled volunteering positions you as an invaluable asset to the causes and organizations you contribute to. For instance, Noah leveraged his UX design talents by volunteering with an educational app aimed at underprivileged youth. His inclusive design approach and empathy for the user experience quickly impressed the founders. Soon, they were introducing Noah to investors and advisors who could potentially fund expanding the app into a fully-fledged ed-tech startup in need of his skills.

Volunteering helps reinforce your narrative as someone committed to a particular domain versus an untested outsider. Jasmine was stuck in corporate law but harbored creative dreams of becoming a novelist and screenwriter. By lending her storytelling abilities to nonprofits in need of human story assets or scriptwriting for promotional videos, she assembled an impressive portfolio. This experience accelerated building credibility when Jasmine subsequently pursued entertainment industry contacts and auditioned for writers' rooms.

Community projects provide an immersive glimpse into the cultures, contexts and stakeholders underpinning your target field. Ethan's aspirations were in social entrepreneurship and sustainabile business - so he embedded himself in local urban gardening and food justice initiatives. This allowed him to understand the challenges and needs of community organizers in ways he'd never grasp from an office. Those grounded perspectives and connections proved invaluable when he launched his own farm-to-food truck venture.

Donating your time and talents doesn't just help worthy causes - it's an unreplicable opportunity to stress-test your fit and passion for a new vocation. For example, Ben volunteered as an EMT before committing to medical school, ensuring he could handle the intense emotional tolls and tempo of emergency response work. While Helena spent a summer assisting indigenous craftswomen to affirm her calling towards ethical fashion and textile preservation before overhauling her design career.

More than any resume bullet or portfolio piece, walking the walk through skilled volunteering showcases your authentic investment in an arena. It allows you to convert theoretical passion into embodied experience while cultivating a network of collaborators equally committed to positive impact. An undeniably priceless value-add when networking your way into a new, meaningful career.

## Social Media Groups and Forums: Your Digital Watering Holes

In our hyper-connected era, some of the most vibrant communities exist not in any physical space but rather the buzzing digital realm. By tapping into the right online forums, social media groups, and other virtual gathering spots, you gain unprecedented access to your new industry's heartbeat.

These platforms are the modern-day watering holes where professionals convene to discuss emerging trends, debate best practices, troubleshoot challenges, and forge new connections around shared experiences. And you'd be remiss not to belly up to the bar and soak up the insights.

My client Yvonne immersed herself in the r/graphic_design subreddit as well as numerous Discord servers during her transition from marketing manager to creative director. Not only did these hangouts provide a constant stream of inspiration and cutting-edge design discourse, she was able to directly interact with the field's top artists and influential voices.

Within these forums, Yvonne would critique others' work, offer feedback when solicited, and share tactics that worked for her own creative process. This authentic value-adding allowed her to very publicly demonstrate her expertise and commitment to the craft. She soon cultivated a reputation as an insightful up-and-coming designer, which opened doors to paid freelance work while building her portfolio.

Meanwhile, Brandon took a more observational approach by joining private Facebook Groups and Slack channels centered around sustainable architecture and urban planning. He absorbed as much as possible through watching discussions unfold - using this recon to identify niche areas of opportunity and who the key players were shaping discourse. This strategy illuminated areas of passion like biophilic design and permaculture that helped niche his focus for a smoother pivot into the green building ecosystem.

These online colonies aren't just rich knowledge repositories though - they're unparalleled networking avenues to make connections. LinkedIn Groups are perfect for breaking the ice with shared interests before attempting to connect more directly. My client Tanya initiated multiple rapport-building conversations through engaging posts within a UX Research & Strategy Group, leading to virtual coffee chats that soon materialized into contract opportunities.

The intimacy and interactivity of these digital spaces allows you to very strategically present your professional brand persona. Gradually build authority and credibility on key topics aligned with your goals. Let curiosity and inquiries guide authentic relationship building. Approach communities with an ethos of generosity - share insights without expectation and you'll be amazed at the connections and opportunities naturally coalescing around you.

From Reddit forums rife with unfiltered dialogue to the curated atmosphere of private Slack channels, embracing these virtual networking venues provides an accessible on-ramp for transitioning into any new scene. You just have to learn the distinct ethos and unwritten rules for respectfully establishing a presence without being disruptive. Once you acquire a knack for engaging, an entirely new world of networking awaits at your fingertips.

Follow Up and Stay Connected: Relationships are Renewable Resources
The most powerful networking is rooted in steadily cultivating authentic, long-term relationships. Making initial connections at events or through introductions is just the first step - consistent follow-up and mutual support is what transforms embryonic bonds into career-propelling forces.

Too often, I see people squander promising leads by failing to take those crucial next steps after an exciting encounter. A basic thank you note or follow-up message to continue the dialogue can make all the difference in ensuring you remain top-of-mind.

Hannah was brilliant about collecting contacts at industry conferences relevant to her UX goals. But her transition stagnated until we implemented a bulletproof follow-up system. Within 24-48 hours after each event, she'd draft personal emails referencing specific moments or insights from their conversations to jog memories. She'd share additional thoughts or resources while proposing a casual meet-up, call, or a next step to continue building rapport.

This level of attentiveness speaks volumes by demonstrating your networking intentions are sincere rather than treating that initial chat as a disposable transaction. It's a simple gesture that positions you as a respectful relationship-builder committed to generosity.

Those thoughtful follow-ups often blossomed into informal coffee meetings or even job interviews as bonds deepened. Sustaining top-of-mind relevance is so critical when people are inundated with distractions and options. Her persistence and reliability made her an undeniable asset others wanted to remain connected to.

On the flip side, good networkers also seek ways to provide continued value to their connections without any expectation of reciprocation. This generosity of spirit reinforces your personal brand.

Nancy made it a habit to share news articles, podcast episodes, or online courses she encountered that specific contacts would appreciate based on their interests or goals. These gestures demonstrated she was continuously looking out for ways to help them while keeping lines of communication open. People naturally gravitate to cultivating stronger ties with someone so thoughtful.

This level of relationship nurturing takes consistent effort and disciplined systems for cataloging your interactions. But put in the work and you tap into a renewable, evergreen resource for your career transition and future endeavors. Those you start investing in now could bring exponential value years down the line through referrals, collaborations, or timely advice when you least expect it.

The most successful people understand the power of planting consistent seeds across their network over time. With intentional nurturing through quality follow-up and support, today's casual business card communication can blossom into tomorrow's transformational professional partnership. Stay connected, nourish the soil, and bear the fruits of abundant relationships.

Give Before You Receive: Plant Seeds of Generosity to Harvest Abundance
One of the most common pitfalls I encounter with people beginning to network is approaching it through a mindset of scarcity and self-interest. They attend events or pursue connections fueled by an underlying "What can I get out of this?" agenda that can inadvertently close more doors than it opens.

The inverse - operating from a perspective of generosity where your mindset is "How can I provide value?" - is not only better professional etiquette, it's a far more effective strategy for manifesting long-term relationship riches.

Marcus struggled to break into the hyper-insular Silicon Valley VC and startup investment universe. No matter how many pitch events or meetups he attended, he gave off a "Please fund my venture!" vibe that was consistently met with a polite but tepid reception. It wasn't until he flipped his focus to positioning himself as a resource conduit - sharing deal flow, making warm intros, gratitude-spreading success stories - that his networking efforts began unlocking previously closed doors.

By leading interactions with an appreciative curiosity about others' goals and looking for ways to facilitate wins through connections or insights, Marcus redefined himself as an impact multiplier. This reframed mindset transformed his presence from one of transactional desperation to being seen as an embedded asset within the very ecosystem he wished to thrive in.

You'd be surprised by how simple yet profound a basic mental reset towards generosity can be for accelerating networking momentum. Former coaching clients have secured career milestones simply by making genuine efforts to support others' objectives without any quid pro quo motive.

For example, Emma wanted to transition into a product management role but lacked direct experience. However, she consistently showed up to her industry Slack group and private forums to offer enthusiastic feedback and developmental suggestions whenever others would post projects for feedback. Her thoughtful ideas and encouraging tone quickly built her reputation as someone worth looping in on ideation sessions and user research panels, despite a lack of formal credentials.

Emma reinvented herself as a substantive value-adder and the ecosystem rewarded her with stretch opportunities and relationships that eventually landed her a product management role.

Generosity is also contagious in the best way. Once you operate from that abundance mindset seeding good faith into your network, you'll be amazed how often the favor gets reciprocated by others inspired to pay it forward. I witnessed this firsthand recently as a client expertly guided a mentee through crafting an eye-catching resume and portfolio for an internship the mentee was striving for. Unprompted, the mentee then spent hours creating tutorial videos on the very design tools they had mastered to save their mentor time later on.

Those who understand the immense power of collaborative networking through mutual support gain access to a self-perpetuating cycle of professional uplift. By making yourself an embodiment of consistent generosity, you develop the type of giving-focused relationships people feel honored to nurture in kind. It triggers a resonance that rapidly multiplies positive returns on both sides.

Ultimately, networking is a long game of continual relationship cultivation. Unsurprisingly, those contributing the most value upfront without hesitation tend to become recipients of an incredible windfall through powerful bonds formed over years. Focusing on what you can provide rather than take initiates a harmonious frequency primed to deliver incredible career abundance when you need it most.

# Mentorship and Guidance: Learn to See Your Blind Spots

Even with diligent self-assessment and research, there will invariably be gaps in knowledge and blind spots when heading into uncharted career territory. This is where proactively seeking out mentors can prove invaluable - their experience and seasoned wisdom can shine a light on the areas you don't even realize you're overlooking.

Ruta saw the need for guidance as she plotted her transition from corporate marketing leader to independent brand strategist. To her, pivoting felt like flying blind without an experienced copilot to navigate the turbulence. To compensate, she assembled an advisory "cabinet" comprised of mentors who could speak to various aspects of being a solopreneur.

For big-picture strategy and positioning, she convened monthly with a former CMO who had built and sold her own agency. This mentor helped Arianna hone her services and packages to meet an unmet market need. Meanwhile, an entrepreneurially-minded accountant friend provided priceless tips for tax optimization, cash flow management, and the tech stack needed to run a lean operation. Her longtime creative director colleague role-played countless positioning discussions to refine Arianna's unique selling proposition.

By piecing together different mentors' complementary insights, Arianna crafted a comprehensive transition roadmap she may have missed with any singular perspective.

Creating a mentor tribe allows you to collate substantive guidance tailored to your own interests and goals. Na-Tasha assembled a "career board of advisors" when she started a hospitality-focused recruiting firm. She met separately with veteran executive recruiters, hoteliers, restaurant owners, and boutique agency founders to understand the differing implications for her business model. Their diverse vantage points revealed risks and opportunities Na-Tasha may have overlooked through any single lens.

Smart mentee-mentor relationships don't just flow one way either. The most impactful mentorship is rooted in mutual exchange and reciprocal accountability.

Take Jack, who sought wisdom from former colleagues in the renewable energy sectors he aspired to work in. In addition to the advice he received for upskilling and licensing requirements, he also provided his mentors with instrumental research into new green building materials, policy updates, or emerging sustainability funds. This positioning as a knowledgeable peer allowed Jack to fast-track his transition by demonstrating a commitment to the industry's evolution through reciprocal value creation.

Don't underestimate the impact even informal mentorship connections can facilitate. One engaged conversation with an industry trailblazer can instantly reframe your mindset in profound ways.

I watched one mentor forever shift a client's perspective in under an hour. Hearing this innovation leader speak candidly about future skills needs like whole-brain thinking and ethical data stewardship instantly expanded a mentee's perceived opportunity paths away from more linear tech or analytics careers. Her skill development priorities instantly expanded in new directions.

The right mentors don't merely offer advice - they grant you entry into entirely new spheres of awareness, influence, and potential. Each connection exponentially expands the frontiers for your career exploration. Make becoming a dedicated mentee a top priority because often, you don't yet know what you aren't seeing or don't know.

## Unlock Unseen Opportunities by Network Diversely

When focused on breaking into a particular career path, it can be tempting to narrowly concentrate your networking efforts solely on people and communities within that precise professional sphere. But by limiting your efforts to such an insular crowd, you inevitably restrict your exposure to new ideas, unexpected connections, and outside-the-box opportunities that could potentially reshape your trajectory for the better.

I learned this lesson through working with Marcus who had his sights set on product management roles within major tech firms. For months, his networking activities revolved around connecting with product leaders, attending product-centric events, and trying to intimately understand that world. What Marcus didn't realize was that he was inadvertently closing himself off from diversity of thought that could have opened entirely new avenues.

It wasn't until Marcus grabbed coffee with an old friend who worked in an unrelated nonprofit arena that everything changed. In catching up, his pal mentioned a new civic tech initiative focused on using modern digital product design to improve community services and engagement. A light bulb went off for Marcus as he recognized his product skills could translate beautifully into this fascinating social impact space he'd never considered. All it took was one conversation outside his narrow industry networking tunnel to make him aware of a profession that activated both his professional passions and personal values in ways he'd missed while myopically chasing FAANG roles. Marcus quickly pivoted his transition plan and is now thriving in an uplifting career path he may have completely overlooked otherwise.

This experience taught me to encourage clients to prioritize networking diversely across all their existing connections - embracing the "strength of weak ties" philosophy. You never know when a former classmate, an old family friend, or the most peripheral contact may randomly unlock an amazing opportunity by exposing you to something totally off your radar. Take my client Natalie, who reached out to her old high school theater crew for career advice as she weighed pursuing a more creative profession. She assumed they'd be useless for networking given their artistic backgrounds differed from her corporate marketing past. However, the conversations opened her eyes to the thriving voice-over industry and the potential to merge her love of improv with her communications skills. Now Natalie is building an incredibly fulfilling career path straddling creative voice work while still consulting on brand strategy.

Even networking "one degree" outside your target industry can spark revelations. Blake was singularly focused on real estate development, so he met with developers, architects, construction managers, asset managers - anyone adjacent to that orbit. It wasn't until he spoke with an urban farmer that Blake's perspectives expanded. Hearing this entrepreneur's philosophy around sustainable land usage and placemaking added an important dimension Blake realized was missing in his development mindset. It motivated him to specialize in green residential projects going forward.

Our networks are just one aspect of life where prioritizing diversity drives exponentially more innovation and growth. In your career transition, chase breadth over depth of exposure. The most seemingly irrelevant person today could be the one introducing you to an opportunity that repositions your entire future in an undiscovered direction.

Diverse networking naturally facilitates more nuanced problem-solving, open-mindedness to new possibilities, and unexpected synergies you'd otherwise miss. So fight the instinct to inhabit an insular social echo chamber just because you think it's most relevant to your goals. Invest in building a vibrant web of varied connections across all walks of life. The further you radiate and the more divergent perspectives you welcome, the more likely you'll encounter an idea that evolves your path beyond anything you could initially envisage.

## Manage Your Online Presence: Craft Your Digital Calling Card

In today's hyper-connected world, your online footprint serves as a powerful modern resume and networking tool that can propel or undermine your career transition. The way you show up across digital channels communicates signals about your professional identity, subject matter expertise, and overall personal brand narrative.

For most people, auditing and optimizing their online presence is one of the first exercises to tackle. Take a hard look at everything from your LinkedIn profile and X activity to personal websites and robust thought-leadership content like blogs and podcasts. The goal is to architect an integrated, public-facing identity tighty aligned with your new career aspirations.

Jessica was pivoting from a corporate marketing role into independent consulting. Her LinkedIn profile was a bit outdated, still featuring primarily her previous full-time work experience. By giving it a major overhaul - updating her headline, about section, featured content, and skills, we positioned her as an experienced brand strategist and creative campaign advisor for established startups and entrepreneurs.

To reinforce this narrative, Jessica began sharing a mix of trends commentary and curated industry articles across LinkedIn and X using hashtags relevant to her niche consulting focus. This allowed her to start attracting and engaging her ideal target audience with insights and thought leadership related to her new services.

This proactive content creation and audience-building laid the important groundwork for attracting potential clients, followers, collaborators, and those who can amplify your new brand. Ethan landed his first big consulting engagement for a national nonprofit simply from an executive following his LinkedIn commentary and being thoroughly impressed with his strategic mind around multi-channel marketing and donor audience segmentation.

It's not just about written content either - many people create portfolios on sites like YouTube, Instagram, TikTok, and Behance to showcase visual representations of their abilities. For example, design and creative professionals share case studies chronicling their processes from concept development to final execution.

Maintaining an active and purposeful presence on relevant forums and community platforms is equally vital. Marissa built a strong reputation as an emerging UX authority on Reddit, Quora, Discord, and a few private Slack groups by consistently contributing insightful advice, design critiques, and industry commentary. Several companies ended up recruiting Marissa for roles after observing and being impressed with her generous expertise sharing.

When managed with intention, your digital footprint amplifies your visibility and positions you as an invaluable resource within your desired professional circles. It allows your voice and personal brand narrative to be a beacon that attracts relevant connections and opportunities.

Of course, you also have to be mindful of inconsistencies or any presence that could undermine your narrative goals. People should delete old accounts, remove questionable content, privatize personal pages, and carefully audit privacy settings across platforms during transitions.

Cleaning up your digital reputation is equally as important as amplifying the presence you wish to cultivate.

Become intentional about the signals you're sending out. With purposeful content curation, community participation, and holistic personal branding, you can manifest your desired career through the pull of your digital gravity.

## Build Your Elevator Pitch: Your 30-Second Calling Card

The ability to clearly and concisely introduce yourself - ambitions, background, and all - is very important. After all, you'll encounter countless spontaneous networking scenarios where having a punchy, compelling elevator pitch can be the difference between forging a new connection or being forgotten.

At its core, your transition elevator pitch should pique curiosity about your unique professional journey and future goals, positioning you as an intriguing person someone should want to keep talking to. It acts as your commercial, conveying the crucial highlights of your story's plot and leaving the audience hungry for more episodes.

Alex was transitioning from a technical role in cybersecurity towards becoming a professional speaker and author on the topic of digital privacy rights. His pitch was gold:

"I used to be one of the 'white hat' hackers companies hired to stress test their firewalls and identify vulnerabilities. But after seeing the expansive ways consumer data gets harvested and abused by corporations and government entities alike, I realized my skills could create more impact by educating everyday people on safeguarding their digital freedoms."

With just a few crisp sentences, Alex adroitly painted a compelling vision of his unusual background, ethical awakening, and the makings of a captivating personal brand. Sharing this tightly scripted intro allowed him to consistently control the narrative when meeting new people who instantly wanted to learn more.

While streamlined and polished, your pitch shouldn't read like a rigid corporate monologue either. You want an authentic, conversational tone that highlights your dynamic personality too. My client Jasmine mastered this by leaning into her playfulness:

"Former math whiz who 'rebelled' by becoming a globe-trotting travel writer and photographer. Think Human Papillon but with fewer prison breaks and more extraordinary pastries eaten."

In under 20 seconds, Jasmine's cheeky pitch establishes a clear outline of her story arc from analytical roots to creative awakening. The self-deprecating humor injected an affable warmth certain to disarm any new connection and spark an engaging dialogue.

For many, the pitch's most vital goal is conveying your aspirational future as vividly as your resume bullet points. Like with Ethan:

"I fell in love with human-centered product management after getting a taste at my last startup. I'm now dedicating myself to the craft of creating impactful digital experiences and tools for underserved communities like the one I grew up in."

While succinct in its delivery, Ethan's pitch is powerfully evocative in expressing his empathetic motivations and the niche domain he envisions himself working within. It leaves you understanding the "why" behind his transition which facilitates natural relationship-building dialogue about his experience or philosophy.

At its best, an elevator pitch is your punchy personal movie trailer - offering just enough of a strategic preview about where you've been, where you're headed, and why someone should feel compelled to buy a ticket to your full show. By devoting focus to tightly scripting these 30-second calling cards, you'll ensure memorable introductions that initiate engaging conversations and meaningful new connections.

I have a video at www.JobSearch.Community that will offer you a model for creating a great one for yourself.

For example, mine is "People hire me for no BS job search coaching and career advice globally because I make the process of finding a new job and succeeding in it much easier."

It is a powerful representation of me and my work. Unlike so many I hear that make me want to take a shower after hearing them, mine is an honest representation of my work with people.

To sum up, as you immerse yourself in networking activities, constantly remind yourself that the ultimate goal transcends accumulating new contacts, whether in person or on LinkedIn, or circulating business cards that will be tossed in a drawer never to be seen again, or thrown out. Especially when attempting the personal reinvention of a career transition, the real prize lies in cultivating a curated inner circle of quality relationships rooted in mutual understanding, support, and authentic human exchange.

Too often we can get seduced by a mindset of MORE - prioritizing volume without discernment. But an overstuffed digital Rolodex or calendar of transactional coffee meetings ultimately rings hollow if you're not fostering genuine bonds with those who can enrich your journey through empathy, trust, and collaborative energy.

Consider the person who joined every professional association related to her new field, and while her organization membership list looked impressive on paper, she remained an anonymous face who never showed up or contributed unique value. She missed myriad opportunities to activate those expensive association investments by forging substantive relationships through consistently engaged presence and vulnerability.

In stark contrast were clients like Sumaira, who strategically focused on just a handful of niche local communities where her passion for ethical fashion and sustainable textile innovation could shine. By generously sharing her experiences and posing thoughtful questions, Sumaira quickly distinguished herself as a curious thought leader. These comparatively tiny networks became fertile soil for mentors to blossom, collaborators to take root, and previously unimaginable opportunities to present themselves through the warmth of personal connections.

Deep professional bonds cultivate intangible benefits like a supportive psychological safety net during stressful career growing pains. I saw firsthand how clients like Malik relied on a few trusted mentors from his new sales opportunities community to buoy his confidence after a discouraging stretch of rejection on the job hunt. Those empathetic listening partnerships and pep talks prevented him from surrendering to impostor syndrome.

When cultivated over a long time, these networking relationships can blossom into profound, legacy-level impacts neither party could have foreseen. For example, Valerie spent years nurturing a humble relationship with a senior regulatory affairs leader through their local biotech professional group. What began as Valerie simply showing up and asking thoughtful questions ultimately inspired her mentor to seed a new academic scholarship for women in STEM fields in her honor.

So while dipping your toes into various networking channels and opportunities is advisable, the real sustainable value lies in nurturing a close cohort of quality connections centered on reciprocal growth, truth-sharing, trust, and mutual giving. Those authentic bonds lubricate your career transition and enrich your entire life through the ineffable ways intertwined relationships elevate us to become the fullest versions of ourselves.

This is the art of soulful networking - an eternal process of opening yourself to purposeful human exchange in the humble service of our collective flourishing. It is through generous vulnerability, curiosity, and appreciation for one another's stories where we all feel emboldened to blaze incredible new pathways of change. No transition is a solo journey when you cultivate a diverse coalition walking beside you in solidarity with each brave step forward.

# Step 4:

# Do a Skill Gap Analysis

Transitioning into a new career often involves acquiring new skills or enhancing existing ones. Before embarking on a career change, it's important to take stock of your current capabilities and align them with the requirements of your future role. A skill gap analysis is the process of identifying skills you currently have and those required in your desired career. This step is essential for a successful transition because it provides a roadmap for your professional development, enabling you to focus your efforts on the areas that need improvement.

A comprehensive skill gap analysis not only highlights the missing pieces in your skill set but also reveals your strengths and transferable skills that can be leveraged in your new career. By objectively assessing your current capabilities and expertise, you can avoid wasting time and resources on areas where you already excel, and instead concentrate on bridging the gaps that may hinder your progress.

Moreover, a skill gap analysis is a valuable tool for setting realistic goals and creating a structured plan for acquiring the necessary knowledge and expertise. Whether it involves enrolling in formal education programs, seeking mentorship, or pursuing self-guided learning, a clear understanding of your skill deficiencies will inform your next steps and ensure that your efforts are targeted and effective.

**Start with a Skills Inventory**

The first step in conducting a skill gap analysis is to take a comprehensive inventory of your current skills. This involves creating a detailed list of both your hard and soft skills. Hard skills refer to the technical abilities and/or concrete knowledge specific to a job or industry, while soft skills encompass interpersonal traits, communication abilities, and problem-solving capabilities.

For example, hard skills would include:

- Programming languages (e.g., Python, Java, C++)
- Data analysis tools (e.g., SQL, Tableau, Excel)
- Design software (e.g., Adobe Creative Suite, AutoCAD)
- Project management methodologies (e.g., Agile, Scrum)
- Foreign languages
- Accounting and financial modeling

Soft skills would include:

- Communication (written and verbal)
- Teamwork and collaboration
- Time management
- Critical thinking and problem-solving
- Adaptability and flexibility
- Leadership and mentoring

To create your skills inventory, reflect on your educational background, work experiences, certifications, and any other relevant training or activities. Don't limit yourself to just professional experiences; consider transferable skills gained through volunteering, hobbies, or personal projects.

Be as specific as possible when listing your skills. For instance, instead of simply stating "programming," specify the languages and frameworks you're proficient in, such as "Python (NumPy, Pandas, Matplotlib)" or "Java (Spring, Hibernate)."

It's also helpful to rank your skills based on your level of proficiency, using a consistent scale (e.g., beginner, intermediate, advanced, expert). This will provide a more accurate picture of your current capabilities and help identify areas where you may need further development.

Remember, this skills inventory is a living document that should be regularly updated as you acquire new skills or enhance existing ones throughout your career journey.

## Research Your Target Career

Once you have a comprehensive list of your current skills, the next step is to research the career or careers you're considering a transition into. This will give you a clear understanding of the specific skills and qualifications required for success in that field. By comparing your existing skills with the demanded competencies, you'll identify potential gaps and areas where you need further development.

Start by examining job descriptions for roles that interest you. These descriptions often provide a detailed list of the necessary hard and soft skills, educational requirements, certifications, and experience levels. Pay close attention to the qualifications that are consistently mentioned across multiple job postings, as these are likely to be essential for the role.

For example, if you're interested in transitioning into a data analyst role, you might notice that skills like SQL, Python or R programming, statistical analysis, data visualization, and problem-solving are frequently listed as requirements.

In addition to job descriptions, industry websites, professional associations, and online forums can be valuable resources for gaining insights into your target career. These often provide information on the latest trends, best practices, and emerging skills within the field.

For instance, if you're exploring a career in digital marketing, visiting websites like the American Marketing Association or following industry influencers on social media can help you stay updated on the latest tools, strategies, and certifications that are in demand.

Furthermore, consider reaching out to professionals currently working in your desired field. Informational interviews or job shadowing opportunities can provide first-hand accounts of the day-to-day responsibilities, challenges, and skills required in that role.

Samantha, a former teacher, decided to transition into instructional design. She researched job descriptions and discovered that skills like e-learning authoring tools, learning management systems, and instructional design models were essential. She then attended virtual meetups and connected with instructional designers on LinkedIn, who shared insights on the importance of skills like project management and multimedia development. By combining research from various sources, you'll get a well-rounded understanding of the skills and qualifications needed for your target career, enabling you to identify gaps in your current skill set and develop a plan to bridge them effectively.

**Identify Transferable Skills**

As you research the requirements for your desired career, it's important to recognize that not all of your current skills will be irrelevant. In fact, many of the skills you've acquired through your previous experiences can be effectively transferred and applied to your new role. Identifying these transferable skills is crucial, as they can provide a solid foundation on which you can build and supplement with additional, more specialized knowledge.

Transferable skills are not specific to a particular job or industry but are broadly applicable across various fields. Some examples of highly transferable skills include:

Communication (written and verbal)
Problem-solving and critical thinking
Leadership and team management
Organization and time management
Adaptability and flexibility
Creativity and innovation
Customer service and interpersonal skills

For instance, if you're transitioning from a sales role to a career in human resources, your strong communication and interpersonal skills will be invaluable when you are conducting interviews, facilitating training sessions, and mediating conflicts within the organization.

Alan spent several years working in the hospitality industry as a restaurant manager. When he decided to pursue a career in project management, he realized that his experience leading teams, managing resources, and resolving conflicts could be readily transferred to his new field. These transferable skills allowed him to quickly adapt to the project management environment and focus on acquiring more technical proficiencies specific to the role.

Sarah, a former journalist, transitioned into a content marketing role. While she needed to learn about SEO, social media marketing, and content management systems, her exceptional writing and storytelling abilities – honed through her journalism experience – were highly valued and transferable skills in her new career.

By identifying your transferable skills, you can leverage your existing strengths and build upon them, rather than starting from scratch. This not only streamlines your career transition process but also sets you apart from other candidates who may lack these versatile abilities.

Remember, transferable skills are often the foundation for success in any role, and recognizing them can give you a competitive edge as you embark on your new career journey.

## Prioritize Skills

After identifying the skills you need to learn for your new career and recognizing your transferable abilities, the next step is to prioritize the remaining skills you need to learn. Not all skills carry equal weight Some may be more important than others to find a job and for success in your new role. By prioritizing your skill development, you can focus on the essentials and avoid spreading yourself too thin.

Start by categorizing the skills into different levels of importance, such as:

1. **Essential Skills**: These are the core competencies without which you cannot effectively perform the job. For example, if you're transitioning into a web development career, essential skills might include proficiency in programming languages like HTML, CSS, and JavaScript.

2. **Highly Desirable Skills:** While not absolutely mandatory, these skills are highly valued and can significantly enhance your performance and competitiveness in the field. Continuing the web development example, skills like responsive design, version control (Git), and familiarity with front-end frameworks (React, Angular) could fall into this category.

3. **Nice-to-Have Skills:** These skills can complement your overall skillset but are not critical for entry-level or mid-career roles. In web development, having experience with server-side scripting (Node.js) or mobile app development could be considered nice-to-have skills.

Once you've categorized the skills, prioritize your learning based on the essential skills first. These should be your primary focus as they form the foundation for your new career. Without mastering these core competencies, you may struggle to perform the fundamental work required for your role.

For example, Jessica transitioned from an administrative role to digital marketing. She prioritized learning essential skills like SEO, Google Analytics, and social media marketing because these were critical for understanding and executing digital marketing campaigns. Once she had a solid grasp of these essentials, she then focused on highly desirable skills like email marketing, content creation, and paid advertising strategies.

By prioritizing your skill development, you can ensure that your efforts are concentrated on the areas that will have the most significant impact on your ability to succeed in your new career. This strategic approach not only maximizes the efficiency of your learning but also prevents you from feeling overwhelmed or spreading your resources too thinly across numerous areas.

Remember, skill development is an ongoing process, and as you progress in your new career, you can gradually expand your focus to include additional desirable and complementary skills. Starting with a clear idea of the essential skills needed will lay a solid foundation for your career transition.

## Education and Training

Once you've identified and prioritized the skills you need to pick up, it's crucial to determine the most effective ways to develop those competencies. For some skills, formal education or training may be necessary, while others can be learned through informal methods or practical experience.

Formal Education Options:

- **Degree programs**: If you're transitioning to a career that requires a specific degree, such as engineering, medicine, or law, pursuing a relevant undergraduate or graduate program may be essential.

- **Certification programs:** Many industries offer professional certifications that validate your knowledge and skills in a particular area. Examples include project management (PMP), human resources (PHR), or IT certifications (CISSP, AWS Certified Solutions Architect).

- **Online courses and bootcamps**: These intensive, accelerated programs can provide targeted training in specific skills like coding, data science, or digital marketing.

Michael transitioned from a sales career to becoming a software developer. He enrolled in an online coding bootcamp that provided comprehensive training in programming languages like Python and JavaScript, as well as practical experience through projects and mentorship. The structured program allowed him to quickly learn the essential skills required for entry-level developer roles.

Informal Learning Options:

- **Books and online resources:** For certain skills, self-study through books, tutorials, and online platforms like Coursera, Udemy, or YouTube can be highly effective and cost-efficient.

- **Mentorship and job shadowing:** Connecting with experienced professionals in your future career can provide valuable guidance, insights, and hands-on learning opportunities.

- **Personal projects and freelancing:** Applying your skills through personal projects or freelance work can help you gain practical experience and build a portfolio.

Emily, a former marketing coordinator, wanted to transition into data analysis. While she didn't pursue a formal degree, she dedicated time to self-study through online courses, tutorials, and practice datasets. She also joined online communities and forums to learn from experienced data analysts and ask for feedback on her projects.

When evaluating education and training options, consider the time and financial commitment required. Formal programs often come with a higher cost but can provide structured learning and accreditation. Informal methods are generally more flexible and cost-effective but may require more self-discipline and initiative, as well as less acceptance by employers.

Additionally, explore free or low-cost educational resources, such as public library databases, massive open online courses (MOOCs), or employer-sponsored training programs. Many reputable institutions and organizations offer high-quality educational content at little or no cost.

Remember, continuous learning and skill development are critical for career growth and adaptability in the job market. By carefully evaluating your options and combining formal and informal learning methods, you can acquire the necessary skills efficiently and effectively, paving the way for a successful transition into your desired career.

## Mentorship and Guidance

As you launch your career transition efforts, asking for guidance and advice from professionals already established in your desired field can be invaluable. These individuals possess first-hand knowledge and experience, offering insights that can help you navigate the path to your new career more effectively.

One of the primary benefits of mentorship is gaining a deeper and real-world understanding of the most valuable skills and competencies required for success in your target role. Mentors can share their perspectives on the essential hard skills, technical expertise, and industry-specific knowledge, as well as the critical soft skills that are often overlooked but equally important.

For instance, if you're transitioning into a project management role, a mentor could emphasize the importance of risk management, stakeholder communication, and leadership skills, in addition to proficiency in project management methodologies and tools.

Mentors can also provide recommendations and guidance on the most effective ways to develop the necessary skills. They may suggest specific educational programs, certifications, online resources, or hands-on experiences that can accelerate your learning and skill acquisition.

Stella wanted to transition from a marketing role to a career in user experience (UX) design. She connected with several UX professionals through networking events and online communities. One advised her to enroll in a UX design course to gain a solid foundation in user research, wireframing, and prototyping tools. Another recommended building a portfolio of personal projects to demonstrate her design thinking and problem-solving abilities.

When seeking mentorship, it's essential to consult with multiple professionals rather than relying solely on advice from one person. Each person may have unique perspectives and experiences, and by gathering insights from several sources, you can identify common threads and recommendations that carry more weight.

For example, if multiple people consistently emphasize the importance of a particular certification or skill, it's likely a strong indication that you should prioritize acquiring that competency.

In addition to one-on-one mentorship, consider joining professional associations or attending industry events and conferences. These platforms can provide opportunities to connect with experienced professionals, attend workshops and/or panel discussions, and expand your network within your desired field.

Mentors and industry professionals can offer invaluable guidance and support throughout your career transition. By actively seeking their advice and being receptive to their recommendations, you can gain a deeper understanding of the skills and knowledge required for success, while also benefiting from their experiences and lessons learned along the way.

Checking in with them regularly to keep them informed on your career transition efforts, including why you may have chosen NOT to take their advice is important.

## Skill Development Plan

Once you've identified the skills you need to acquire, prioritized their importance, and gotten advice from mentors and industry professionals, it's time to create a comprehensive plan for developing your skills. A well-structured plan will help you stay focused, organized, and accountable.

Your skill development plan should include the following:

1. **Timelines:** Set realistic timelines for when you aim to achieve specific skill milestones or competency levels. Break down larger goals into smaller, manageable targets to avoid feeling overwhelmed.

2. **Resources:** Identify the resources you'll need to develop each skill, such as educational materials (books, online courses, workshops), software tools, or hands-on projects. List the specific resources you plan to utilize and their associated costs, if any.

3. **Specific Actions:** Outline the specific actions you'll take to acquire or improve each skill. This could include enrolling in a course, completing tutorials, practicing with coding exercises, or seeking out freelance opportunities to gain practical experience.

4. **Checkpoints and Assessments:** Incorporate regular checkpoints to evaluate your progress and assess your skill proficiency. This could involve completing practice tests, obtaining certifications, or receiving feedback from mentors or peers.

Alex transitioned from a customer service role to a career in data analysis. His skill development plan included:

- **Timeline:** Gain proficiency in SQL and data visualization tools within 6 months.

- **Resources:** Online SQL course on Coursera, data analysis books, and free data visualization software like Tableau.

- **Actions:** Complete SQL course assignments, practice with sample datasets, and develop data visualization projects for a portfolio.

- **Checkpoints:** Obtain a SQL certification after 4 months and get feedback on data visualization projects from a mentor. Another example is Sarah, who wanted to transition from a marketing coordinator role to a front-end web development career. Her plan included:

- **Timeline:** Achieve proficiency in HTML, CSS, and JavaScript within 9 months, and learn a front-end framework like React within 12 months.

- **Resources:** Online coding bootcamp, web development books, and coding practice platforms like FreeCodeCamp.

- **Actions:** Complete bootcamp projects, build personal websites or web applications, and participate in coding challenges.

- **Checkpoints:** Receive feedback on coding projects from bootcamp instructors and peers, and create a portfolio of work to showcase skills.

Remember, your skill development plan should be a living document that can be adjusted and refined as you progress. Celebrate your achievements and milestones along the way, and don't be discouraged by setbacks or slippage with meeting your timeline – they are a natural part of the learning process.

By creating a comprehensive and actionable plan, you'll have a roadmap to guide your skill development journey, allowing you to stay focused, motivated, and on track toward your career transition goals.

## Practice and Apply Them

Learning skills through coursework, books, or online resources is an essential first step, but true mastery comes from actively practicing and applying those skills in real-world scenarios. Hands-on experience is invaluable, as it allows you to reinforce your learning, identify areas for improvement, and develop a deeper understanding of how to apply your skills effectively.

Consider projects, internships, or volunteer work to gain hands-on experience and build your skillset.

One approach is to seek out projects or freelance opportunities that align with your desired career. This could involve taking on small freelance gigs, contributing to open-source projects, or creating personal projects to showcase your skills. For example, if you're transitioning into web development, you could build a portfolio website or develop a simple web application to practice your coding abilities.

After completing an online user experience (UX) design course, Judith knew she needed real-world practice to solidify her skills. She volunteered to redesign the website for a local non-profit organization, allowing her to apply her knowledge of user research, wireframing, and prototyping. This project not only strengthened her UX skills but also provided a tangible example of her work for her portfolio."

Internships can also be invaluable to gain practical experience and exposure to a professional environment within your desired field. Many companies offer internship programs specifically designed to provide hands-on training and mentorship. Internships offer a unique chance to apply your skills while learning from experienced professionals.

Jacob had been studying data analytics through online courses and tutorials. He secured a summer internship at a marketing firm to further his skill development. During his internship, he worked alongside experienced data analysts, learning how to clean and analyze real-world datasets, create visualizations, and present insights to stakeholders. This practical experience solidified his understanding of data analysis workflows and prepared him for a full-time role after graduation.

Volunteering can be another avenue for gaining practical experience, particularly if you're transitioning to a career in a non-profit or community-based organization. By volunteering your skills and time, you can contribute to meaningful causes while simultaneously enhancing your abilities.

Volunteering allows you to make a positive impact while developing your skills in a real-world setting.

After completing a project management certification, Emily wanted to put her newly acquired skills into practice. She volunteered to lead a community outreach initiative for a local charity, where she was responsible for organizing events, managing volunteers, and coordinating logistics. This hands-on experience reinforced her project management knowledge and showcased her ability to lead teams and deliver results.

Remember, practicing and applying your skills is an ongoing process, even after transitioning into a new career. Continuously seek out opportunities to challenge yourself, learn from experienced professionals, and refine your abilities. The more you immerse yourself in real-world scenarios, the more confident and proficient you'll become in your new role.

**Feedback and Assessment**

Regularly asking for feedback and assessing your progress is crucial to the skill development journey. It allows you to evaluate the effectiveness of your learning strategies, identify areas that require further improvement, and make necessary adjustments to your skill gap analysis and development plan.

As you engage in hands-on projects, internships, or volunteer work, actively get feedback from mentors, instructors, or experienced professionals in your desired field. Their insights and constructive criticism can provide invaluable guidance on where you excel and where you need to focus your efforts. For instance, Joan was transitioning into a user experience (UX) design career. She regularly shared her wireframes and prototypes with a seasoned UX designer for feedback. This mentor's guidance helped her refine her design thinking and better understand industry best practices.

In addition to external feedback, it's important to conduct regular self-assessments to gauge your progress objectively. This could involve taking practice tests, completing coding challenges, or analyzing the results of your projects or assignments. By honestly evaluating your work, you can identify areas where you have mastered the necessary skills and areas that require further development.

Jacob, the aspiring data analyst, regularly practiced his data cleaning and visualization skills using online datasets. He then compared his work to industry-standard practices, allowing him to identify gaps in his knowledge and areas for improvement, such as advanced statistical techniques or data storytelling.

As you receive feedback and conduct self-assessments, be prepared to make adjustments to your skill gap analysis and development plan. If you're struggling with a particular skill or concept, consider allocating more time or resources to that area, or seeking additional support through mentorship or supplementary learning materials.

Emily, who was transitioning into a project management role, initially struggled with risk management and stakeholder communication. After receiving feedback from her volunteer project leader, she revised her development plan to include additional courses and resources focused on those specific skills.

Regularly reassessing your progress and adapting your plan ensures that you remain on track and continuously refine your approach to skill development. It's also important to celebrate your achievements and milestones along the way, as this can provide motivation and a sense of accomplishment, fueling your determination to continue growing and improving.

By embracing feedback, conducting honest self-assessments, and making adjustments as needed, you can optimize your skill development journey, positioning yourself for success in your desired career transition.

Tapping into the Power of Your Network for Accelerated Skill Development
Acquiring skills as part of a career transition can be accelerated by using your professional network. They can provide a wealth of opportunities for guidance, mentorship, and access to invaluable learning resources. Connecting with individuals who have already mastered the expertise you're striving to attain can significantly accelerate your progress and increase your chances of success.

As Aisha transitioned from a marketing role to a career in data science, her alma mater's alumni network proved instrumental. Through this connection, she met a seasoned data scientist who not only shared insights into the most in-demand skills but also recommended online courses, coding challenges, and industry conferences to attend. This personalized guidance helped her navigate the vast array of learning resources and focus her efforts on the most relevant and effective ones.

Your network can serve as a gateway to mentors who can offer personalized guidance and support throughout your skill development journey. Jacob, the aspiring data analyst, attended local meetup events and connected with seasoned professionals who offered to review his projects and provide constructive criticism, accelerating his learning process and helping him identify areas for improvement.

Moreover, your professional connections can be a source of information about job shadowing, internships, or freelance opportunities that allow you to gain hands-on experience and apply your newly acquired skills in a real-world setting. Emily, who was transitioning into a project management career, leveraged her network to secure a part-time internship at a local technology firm, where she could practice her project management skills while learning from experienced professionals.

Building and maintaining a strong professional network requires effort and intentionality. Attend industry events, join professional associations, and participate in online communities related to your desired career. Engage in meaningful conversations, offer your expertise and support to others, and consistently nurture these connections. Terry actively participated in online design forums, sharing his work and seeking feedback from experienced professionals. This not only allowed him to improve his skills but also expanded his network, leading to potential job opportunities and collaborations.

By actively cultivating and leveraging your professional connections, you gain access to a wealth of knowledge, resources, and opportunities that can significantly accelerate your skill development journey. Your network can provide guidance, support, and practical experiences that complement your formal learning, ensuring a well-rounded and comprehensive approach to acquiring the necessary skills for your desired career transition.

## Stay Up to Date: Embracing Continuous Learning

Staying up to date with industry trends and changing skill demands is essential for maintaining a competitive edge and ensuring long-term success in your new career. As technologies advance, best practices evolve, and market dynamics shift, the skills required for optimal performance are constantly in flux.

Committing to a mindset of continuous learning is crucial for staying ahead of the curve and adapting to the ever-changing requirements of your field. This involves actively seeking out and engaging with industry-specific resources, such as publications, blogs, podcasts, and online communities, to stay informed about the latest developments, emerging tools, and innovative techniques.

For instance, CJ, a UX designer, made it a habit to regularly read design blogs and attend virtual conferences to learn about new design trends, user research methodologies, and cutting-edge prototyping tools. By staying up to date, they were able to continuously refine her skills and incorporate the latest best practices into her work, ensuring her designs remained fresh, user-centric, and aligned with industry standards.

Networking and maintaining strong professional connections can also play a vital role in keeping you informed about shifting skill demands. Engaging with experienced professionals in your field can provide valuable insights into the skills and expertise that are becoming increasingly sought after, allowing you to proactively adapt and develop those competencies.

Dave regularly attended local meetups and engaged with industry experts on social media platforms like LinkedIn. Through these connections, he learned about the growing importance of different skills than those he had experience with. Armed with this knowledge, he was able to prioritize upskilling in these areas, ensuring his skill set remained relevant and competitive.

Additionally, embracing a growth mindset and being open to ongoing skill development is crucial. As industries evolve, new tools, methodologies, and best practices will emerge, requiring a willingness to continuously learn and adapt. Pursue professional development opportunities, such as workshops, certification programs, or online courses, to stay ahead of the curve and maintain a competitive advantage in your new career.

Connie recognized the increasing demand for agile methodologies in her field. She proactively sought out online training and obtained certifications in Agile and Scrum, enhancing her skills and positioning herself as a valuable asset in the rapidly changing project management landscape. To not have done so would have been professional suicide in a few years.

By staying up to date with industry trends, engaging with professional networks, and embracing continuous learning, you can future-proof your career and ensure that your skills remain relevant and in demand. This commitment to ongoing skill development not only enhances your value as a professional but also fosters personal growth, job satisfaction, and long-term career success in your new field.

## Celebrate Successes: Acknowledging Your Milestones on the Path to Your Career Change

The journey of acquiring new skills and transitioning into a new career can be challenging and demanding, requiring dedication, perseverance, and a significant investment of time and effort. Amidst the intense focus on learning and growth, it's essential to pause and recognize your achievements, no matter how small they may seem. Celebrating your successes along the way not only boosts your motivation and confidence but also serves as a reminder of how far you've come and the progress you've made.

Sarah, a former marketing professional, decided to pivot into web development. Initially, the task of learning programming languages and frameworks seemed daunting, but as she diligently worked through online courses and coding challenges, she began to see her skills take shape. When Sarah successfully built her first functional website, she took a moment to revel in her accomplishment, recognizing the countless hours of study and practice that had led her to that milestone.

Similarly, for Michael, a recent graduate who transitioned into data science, the journey was marked by numerous milestones worth celebrating. From completing his first data analysis project to obtaining a coveted industry certification, each achievement reinforced his dedication and fueled his motivation to continue pushing forward.

Celebrating successes doesn't necessarily require grand gestures or elaborate celebrations. It can be as simple as treating yourself to a favorite meal, sharing your accomplishments with loved ones or peers, or taking a well-deserved break to recharge before tackling the next challenge.

Emma made it a practice to acknowledge her progress by updating her professional portfolio with each successful project or certification she completed. This act of documenting her achievements not only provided a sense of pride and accomplishment but also served as a tangible record of her growing skill set.

Recognizing and celebrating your successes along the way also helps to combat feelings of overwhelm or discouragement that can sometimes arise during the skill acquisition process. When faced with setbacks or challenges, reflecting on your previous achievements can serve as a powerful reminder of your capabilities and resilience, helping you regain your motivation and confidence.

Taylor encountered numerous roadblocks while learning new design software and methodologies. However, whenever she felt discouraged, she would revisit her portfolio of successful projects from her previous career, reminding herself of the skills and determination she had already demonstrated.

Ultimately, the journey of skill acquisition and career transition is a marathon, not a sprint. By acknowledging and celebrating your milestones, big and small, you not only stay motivated and engaged but also cultivate a sense of accomplishment and pride in your personal and professional growth.

Remember, skill gap analysis is not a one-time process but rather an ongoing journey that should accompany you throughout your career transition and beyond. As you progress and immerse yourself deeper into your new field, you'll gain valuable insights and a more nuanced understanding of the intricate skills and competencies required for long-term success.

This heightened awareness may unveil additional areas for growth, prompting you to identify and prioritize the acquisition of supplementary skills or the refinement of existing ones. Embrace this continuous process of self-evaluation and adaptation as an opportunity to stay ahead of the curve and maintain a competitive edge in your chosen profession.

Regularly revisiting your skill gap analysis allows you to recalibrate your development plan, ensuring that your efforts remain aligned with the ever-evolving demands of your industry. It enables you to pivot and adjust your learning trajectory as needed, preventing stagnation and fostering a mindset of lifelong learning – an invaluable asset in today's rapidly changing job market.

Moreover, this ongoing skill gap analysis empowers you to anticipate future trends and emerging technologies, equipping you with the foresight to proactively develop the necessary skills before they become essential prerequisites in your field. By staying ahead of the curve, you'll not only increase your chances of excelling in your new career but also position yourself as a valuable asset to potential employers or clients.

This comprehensive and iterative approach to skill gap analysis is instrumental in ensuring that you are well-prepared to excel in your new career. It bridges the divide between your current skill set and the requirements of your desired profession, making your transition smoother, more efficient, and ultimately more successful. Embrace this process as an integral part of your professional journey, and watch as your skills, confidence, and career prospects soar to new heights.

# Step 5:

# Research Your New Career

We live in an era of extraordinary times with access to amazing amounts of information and opinions. For anyone considering a career transition, online research has become an indispensable tool to explore new career paths, understand what they entail, and determine if they could be a good fit. Effectively doing online research can make your career transition smoother and more successful.

The wealth of data and resources available online allows you to go far beyond surface-level job descriptions and requirements. With some diligent searching, you can find insider perspectives from people working in the fields you're interested in, learn about the day-to-day realities of different roles from different people, get a sense of growth prospects, understand compensation levels, and so much more. This step can help you make a more informed decision about which new career direction could be most rewarding and aligns best with your interests, skills, and lifestyle goals.

However, the abundance of information online also means you need to be savvy about separating reputable sources from misinformation or outdated material. Developing targeted search strategies, identifying trustworthy sites and authors, and cross-referencing information from multiple credible sources is imperative. When done well, online research equips you with reliable, comprehensive insights to confidently transition into your next professional chapter.

In this step, we'll cover efficient techniques to search career information online, ways to tap into the wisdom of industry insiders, and how to fact-check and vet the resources you find. You can transform the technology into a powerful career transition ally with the right approach.

## Industry Overview

Start by obtaining a comprehensive overview of your target industry. Search for reputable sources that provide insights into the industry's size, growth trajectory, major players, emerging trends, and disruptive forces at play. This high-level understanding helps you assess if the industry aligns with your interests and has positive prospects.

For instance, when researching a career in renewable energy, you might find reports from the International Energy Agency and industry associations like the American Wind Energy Association. These could reveal that renewables are one of the fastest-growing energy sources globally, fueled by climate change concerns and supportive policies. You'd learn about major companies as well as up-and-comers innovating in areas like energy storage. Reports may highlight technical breakthroughs like improved solar panel efficiency as a key trend driving demand.

In e-commerce, a site like DigitalCommerce360 could orient you to the massive scale of the industry, major retailers like Amazon and Walmart, as well as disruptive forces like the rise of mobile shopping and demand for seamless omnichannel experiences. You'd see data on sustained double-digit annual growth and the competitive battleground emerging between legacy brands and upstart digital natives.

These birds-eye industry views from authoritative sources allow you to understand growth prospects, major players delivering products/services, the competitive landscape, and technical or consumer forces disrupting business as usual. With this context, you can evaluate if the industry inspires you before diving deeper into potential career paths within it.

## Job Market Analysis

After getting an industry overview, drill down into analyzing the actual job market within your chosen field. Look for data on current open job listings, demand projections for specific roles over the next 5-10 years, and where the geographic hotspots are for hiring in this line of work. Government labor statistics, job search engines, and authoritative career information sites can provide invaluable insights.

For example, if exploring healthcare administration roles, you could consult the U.S. Bureau of Labor Statistics website. You may find data projecting 32% employment growth for medical and health services managers through 2030 - much faster than the average. The BLS breaks this down by specific roles like nursing home administrators and clinical managers. You'd see the states with the highest employment levels, like California, Texas, and New York.

Drilling deeper into job search sites like Indeed, Monster or Glassdoor could reveal thousands of active job listings matching your criteria. You can analyze the locations with the most openings, whether it's major hospital hubs like Boston or growing job markets like Nashville. You can see actual job descriptions to better understand the skills and experience employers are prioritizing.

If considering pivoting to UX design, sites like Dribbble's job board can give you information about how many companies are actively hiring UX roles. You may find cities like San Francisco, Seattle, and Austin have particularly high demand. Looking at postings could indicate if there's more demand for certain specialized skills.

This granular research ensures your career transition isn't just based on an exciting-sounding field, but data showing there is not substantive demand for the specific roles and skills you want to develop and where those opportunities are concentrated.

**Professional Associations**

As you research a potential career path, don't overlook the value of professional associations and organizations related to that field. These groups can provide insider resources to help you better understand the profession and key trends shaping it. Their offerings frequently may include industry news, educational content, networking events, career resources, and research reports.

For instance, when Monica began exploring a midlife career change to become a financial advisor, she joined the Financial Planning Association (FPA). Through the FPA, she received access to the Journal of Financial

Planning, which helped her stay up-to-date on regulatory changes, investment strategies, and best practices from experienced members. The FPA's regional chapters also hosted networking meetups where Monica could connect with advisors and learn about different firm cultures.

Joshua leveraged the American Marketing Association (AMA) as he transitioned from a sales career to marketing. The AMA offered online training courses on social media marketing and web analytics that helped him build critical skills. He also attended the AMA's annual conference, which featured workshops led by top brand marketers, who shared real-world case studies.

For those interested in project management, the Project Management Institute (PMI) provides access to templates, webinars on agile methodologies, and support for obtaining PMP certification. PMI's local chapters bring together professionals to network and find mentors who can advise on making the career switch.

Beyond skills training, professional associations give you access to troves of industry research reports that can enhance your working knowledge. And their career centers can point you toward open jobs and connect you with recruitment firms. Joining these organizations allows you to immerse yourself in your new professional community.

## Company Research

Once you've identified companies that interest you, dig deeper by thoroughly researching their websites, online profiles, and any public information. The goal is to get a well-rounded understanding of the company's culture, values, business priorities, and work environment. This will help ensure it's a good fit for you and guide how you tailor your resume, portfolio, if appropriate, and prepare for interviews.

For example, when Sue was looking to transition into a marketing role at a major athletic apparel brand, she spent hours poring over the company's website. She studied their "About Us" section to understand the company's history, mission, and core values like sustainability. She browsed the brand's catalogs and marketing campaigns to analyze their brand voice and visual identity.

She also looked for employee profiles and testimonials to get a sense of what the workplace culture was like. Were employees depicted as hardworking and competitive or more focused on work-life balance? This helped her gauge if she'd thrive in that environment. She even identified employees she'd be interested in connecting with on LinkedIn for insider insights.

For Jamal exploring finance companies, researching annual reports and investor presentations helped him understand each firm's business strategies, growth areas, and challenges. One wealth management company seemed focused on digital transformation, while another prioritized aggressive global expansion. This signaled what skills may be most valued in each workplace.

Online reviews from sites like Glassdoor and InHerSight provided another window into company cultures. For instance, reviews may reveal a consulting firm has an intense workaholic culture, while a tech startup has a more casual, dog-friendly office environment. Reading about this firsthand could confirm if it aligns with the lifestyle you want.

Deep company research allows you to determine culture fit, prepare insightful questions for interviews, and tailor your pitch for why you're an ideal person for that particular company. It transforms you from a blind applicant to a knowledgeable, highly interested prospect.

## LinkedIn and Social Media

Social platforms have become indispensable tools for professional networking, joining industry conversations, and conducting inside-out career research. LinkedIn in particular provides powerful capabilities for connecting directly with professionals working in the roles and companies you're targeting.

When Amanda decided to pivot from teaching into the world of corporate learning and development, she immediately updated her LinkedIn profile with her new career interests. She followed eLearning companies like Udemy and Degreed, as well as prominent L&D thought leaders. This allowed her to see trends, open job postings, and insights being shared.

She then joined groups like the Association for Talent Development where she could post questions to tap into the collective knowledge of thousands of L&D practitioners globally. She discovered what skills were in demand, learned about different corporate training philosophies and approaches, and even got feedback on updating her resume.

Perhaps most powerfully, Amanda used LinkedIn's alumni tool to find graduates from her university currently working in corporate L&D roles. She sent outreach messages explaining her career transition goals, and many were willing to have informational interview calls. These first-hand conversations gave Amanda an unvarnished look at the day-to-day work, different L&D specializations, and pathways to break into the field.

Outside of LinkedIn, Amanda monitored relevant X hashtags like #CorporateTraining and #LearningDesign to see what topics and external training providers were being discussed. She joined several private Facebook groups as well to ask more sensitive career questions and get candid crowd-sourced advice.

Social platforms have evolved far beyond just professional networking and socializing. They now can provide a vibrant window into different career realms, allowing you to immerse yourself in the conversations, wisdom, and connections that facilitate a successful professional reinvention.

## Educational Resources

The rise of online learning has created affordable and easily accessible educational resources that can be incredibly valuable when researching and preparing for a career transition. Many universities, colleges, and educational institutions now offer free or low-cost online courses spanning a diverse array of industries and subjects. Taking advantage of these can help fill knowledge gaps, develop new skills, and gain credible industry-specific insights.

For those looking to break into fields like marketing, finance, or entrepreneurship, massive open online courses (MOOCs) from providers like Coursera, edX, and FutureLearn bring high-quality instruction from leading universities. You can take courses on topics like digital marketing analytics, financial modeling, or lean startup principles - all for little to no cost. Having completed relevant courses demonstrates initiative and can better position you for success in your new role.

Platforms like LinkedIn Learning, SkillShare, and Udemy offer gigantic video course libraries taught by industry professionals on more specialized and niche topics. These allow you to affordably access training on focused skills whether it's social media marketing, customer experience design, data visualization, or virtually any other career subject area.

If transitioning into a highly technical or licensed field like software development, project management, or healthcare administration, many prestigious institutions provide lower-cost online certificates and credentialing programs. Offerings from names like Harvard, MIT, and Georgia Tech can give you a professional edge by delivering comprehensive curriculums from world-class instructors.

Beyond courses, educational resources like industry pdf reports, academic journals, and expert-hosted webinars from universities can supplement your self-guided research by providing authoritative perspectives into cutting-edge developments within your target field. You gain access to the latest research and insider knowledge usually only available to enrolled students.

Continuous learning is essential for career success. Taking advantage of the bounty of free and low-cost online educational resources allows you to cost-effectively upskill, gain credentialing, and demonstrate your passion for your new profession.

## Online Forums and Communities

There is a vast ecosystem of online forums, discussion boards, and social media communities dedicated to virtually every industry and professional niche imaginable. Tapping into these vibrant communities can be an invaluable part of your career research process. They provide a direct line to solicit insights from insiders actively working in your target field.

For example, Reddit hosts hundreds of career and industry-specific subredd its like r/accounting, r/sysadmin, r/marketing, and r/projectmanagement. Within these communities, you can read posts and comment threads discussing the latest trends, and getting advice on everything from resume tips to handling tricky workplace situations. You can pose questions to the group and get candid feedback from people with diverse opinions.

Many professions have flagship online communities as well. The iPhone SDK Developer group is a long-running community for iOS developers to discuss coding challenges. There are expansive communities dedicated to data science, UX design, product management, and beyond.

Within these forums, you can join conversations to learn the current hot technologies and methodologies. You may get information about unique career specializations you hadn't considered. Veteran members are often willing to share their firsthand experiences through an "Ask Me Anything" style Q&A. Or you can search archives to see how community discussions evolve over time on particular topics.

In addition to traditional web forums, don't overlook the value of social media groups on Facebook, LinkedIn, and others. These communities allow you to seamlessly tap into a feed of fresh, up-to-date dialogue from industry professionals around the world at any moment.

While not as formal as paid training courses, online communities can provide an intimate, unvarnished view directly from the trenches. You gain exposure to the vernacular, pain points, ongoing debates, and evolving best practices that textbooks or corporate websites don't capture. This insider access is invaluable when vetting a potential new field.

## Blogs, Podcasts, and YouTube Channels

Many industry professionals and thought leaders share their expertise, advice, and experiences through blogs, podcasts, and video channels. These can be goldmines of practical, real-world insights when researching potential new career paths.

Seek out popular blogs centered around your target industry or roles of interest. Many seasoned professionals have YouTube channels sharing day-in-the-life vlogs, interviewing tips, or tutorials related to their work. A project manager may share videos breaking down different methodologies. A graphic designer could offer a look into their creative process. These visual snapshots can help demystify what certain roles actually entail.

Podcasts have exploded in popularity as well, with highly-niched shows allowing you to metaphorically "pull up a chair" to candid conversations in any industry Shows provide entertaining and informative soundtracks into their respective fields.

Beyond providing a window into potential careers, blogs, podcasts and YouTube can expose you to buzzwords, publications, conferences, and personalities that are influential in a given space. You may discover tools, books, or thinkers that help accelerate your learning curve.

Many bloggers, podcasters, and YouTubers monetize their content through sponsors, online courses, or books - providing affordable supplemental training and educational materials. Their archives can serve as free libraries on virtually any career topic imaginable.

While formal job descriptions only skim the surface, these firsthand accounts from passionate insiders allow you to truly understand the skills, knowledge, and personalities that tend to flourish in different vocational areas. With so much content just a search away, you can efficiently immerse yourself in your prospective field's culture and community.

## News and Publications

To truly immerse yourself in your prospective new career, stay updated on the latest industry news, developments, and forward-looking analysis. Subscribing to influential trade publications, magazines, journals, and newsletters allows you to view your field of interest through an insider's lens.

When Gabriela began exploring a midlife career pivot from finance into ESG (environmental, social, governance) investing, she immediately subscribed to publications like Environmental Finance and Responsible Investor. Their articles exposed her to emerging regulations, stakeholder initiatives, new sustainability reporting frameworks, and fund ratings/rankings. She also started to learn how to speak in the language of her new chosen field.

By reading interviews with chief sustainability officers and ESG portfolio managers, Gabriela gained insights into their priorities, challenges, and credentials. She learned about issues like greenwashing and ESG data gaps before even starting to try to enter the field. This knowledge helped her determine which skills would be most valued.

For Seth, a software developer investigating transitioning into cybersecurity, he turned to resources like ThreatPost and DarkReading. These sources provided a constant stream of information about the latest threat vectors, attack methodologies, vulnerability analyses and security solutions.

He would chart the rise of particular malware strains or hacker groups making headlines. He saw which companies and cybersecurity providers were leading the response efforts. The analyses and industry commentaries helped Seth understand roles like penetration testing, incident response, and secure coding practices that would be in high demand.

Rajesh, an accountant intrigued by data science and AI, found different publications instrumental. Their articles explored new machine learning techniques, natural language processing applications, and companies gaining competitive advantages through data-driven decision-making.

By reading about data scientists partnering with business teams to solve challenges, he gained an appreciation for the hybrid technical/problem-solving skillset required. He could see the immense potential for roles combining data fluency, quantitative methods, and business acumen.

Keeping a pulse on industry publications, whether digital, print, or podcasts, ensures you don't only understand the current state of a field, but where it's headed. The analyses and trendspotting empower you to make an informed decision about your future career path's growth trajectory and opportunity areas. It allows you to learn, get ahead of the curve, and anticipate the future rather than just react to it.

## Reviews and Testimonials

While job descriptions and company overviews provide one perspective, reading candid reviews and testimonials from people actively working in your area(s) of interest can offer a much more nuanced, warts-and-all view. These accounts can shed light on the daily realities, challenges, workplace cultures, and personal experiences associated with different vocations.

When Kyle began exploring careers in renewable energy after being downsized from oil and gas, he scoured job review sites like Glassdoor and Indeed. For a wind turbine technician role he was considering, he read about the exciting but grueling working conditions - from scaling great heights, to being exposed to extreme weather, to long stretches away from home.

Counterbalancing that were reviews highlighting the meaningful environmental impact, cutting-edge technology utilized, and tight-knit workplace camaraderie. He gained a three-dimensional perspective - the role's arduous physical and lifestyle demands, but also its profound upsides.

Francesca had her sights set on becoming an event planner, dreaming of the creativity and energy of bringing people together. However, testimonials from experienced planners opened her eyes to some harsh realities she hadn't considered - the round-the-clock working hours leading up to events, the endless budget pressures, and the never-ending demands of high-maintenance clients.

At the same time, Francesca read about the rush of executing a seamless high-profile gala and building connections across industries. She could weigh the intense stressors against the gratification of producing remarkable shared experiences.

Maya, a finance analyst curious about product management, tapped into PM community forums like ProductPlan's "Roadmap" which revealed eye-opening insider views. Seasoned product managers detailed the constant tug-of-war between an avalanche of incoming customer requests and the realities of managing development roadmaps and resource constraints.

While it seemed exciting to serve as the critical translator between users and developers, PMs frequently had to make tough prioritization calls that disappointed many stakeholders. These balanced perspectives allowed Maya to appreciate the multi-faceted challenges and necessity for strategic decision-making that work entailed.

By accessing true stories and advice from people familiar with different career realities, you can develop a well-rounded understanding before leaping. Reviews and testimonials humanize roles beyond just skills requirements and growth prospects. They equip you with invaluable foreknowledge of the cultural, personal, and psychological demands to thrive in your next professional chapter.

## Market Research Reports

To obtain a comprehensive and data-driven understanding of industry trends, competitive landscapes, emerging opportunities and potential challenges, it can be invaluable to access professional market research reports. These in-depth analyses provide extensive data, forecasting models, and expert insights that go far beyond what's available through free online research alone.

While market research reports from leading firms like Gartner, IDC, Forrester and others can come with substantial price tags, they offer an unparalleled level of rigor and credible third-party perspective. Analysts combine primary research like surveying professionals and conducting interviews, with mining public data sources, proprietary methodologies, and decades of industry knowledge.

The result is a holistic, meticulously researched view into market sizes, growth projections, buyer behavior analysis, assessment of disruptive forces, vendor evaluations, and identification of whitespace opportunities. You gain quantification around areas of future demand aligned to your skills, rather than just anecdotal evidence.

For those unable to purchase pricey reports, checking if your local public or university library provides subscriptions to research databases can be an option. Even seeking out free excerpts, summaries, and webinars from research firms can still yield useful high-level intelligence to inform your career decisions.

Either way, tapping into the analytics and foresight from seasoned market research professionals ensures you enter your new field with a grounded, numbers-backed understanding of the playing field. You can optimize your skillset and professional development for the areas forecasted for the greatest opportunity. Often, these reports will equip you with ammunition to persuasively convey your value to prospective employers and differentiate yourself in interviews.

The US Bureau of Labor Statistics (www.bls.gov) offers useful information about jobs and industries in its industries. Once at the website, search for The Occupational Outlook, Publications Occupational Outlook Handbook for more about specific fields and federal government projections for jobs in those fields.

In addition, many online brokerage accounts offer research into particular firms and their prospects.

While free online research casts a wide net, complementing it with the focused, robust analysis through market research studies allows you to pursue your career pivot armed with substantive data to execute a strategic, future-proof transition.

## Competitive Analysis

An often overlooked but a very valuable component of career transition research is taking the time to closely study those who are already succeeding in the roles and industries you aspire to join. Identify standout professionals and thought leaders in your target field, then thoroughly analyze their backgrounds, credentials, skillsets, and career trajectories.

For Nick, who was pivoting from finance into product marketing for software companies, he made a list of product marketers at top tech firms whose blogs and LinkedIn posts impressed him with their insights. He spent hours meticulously deconstructing their career histories and skill sets.

He noticed that while a business or marketing degree was fairly common, many product marketers had unexpected backgrounds in areas like communications, journalism, or user experience. He realized skills like storytelling, customer empathy, and technical writing abilities were particularly prized. This guided him to beef up his portfolio with writing samples highlighting those strengths.

Lily, an ad agency creative director exploring a transition into the hot field of influencer marketing, identified a handful of pioneers who had built successful personal brands and businesses. In studying their paths, Lily learned many had complemented their creative talents with entrepreneurial skills like contract negotiation, monetization strategies, production coordinating, and analytical marketing chops.

Crucially, Lily gained an appreciation for just how much commitment and business savvy were required beyond just creating compelling content. It showed this career had depth far beyond what was portrayed by superficial Instagram influencers.

For software developer Marcus, he was keen to work in machine learning after taking online courses. By closely following ML engineers, researchers, and leaders, Marcus saw that hands-on experience applying algorithms to real-world datasets was more valued by employers than academic credentials alone.

He grew his GitHub portfolio showcasing different ML models he'd built, participated in Kaggle competitions, polished skills like exploratory data analysis, model deployment, and quantitative soft skills like presenting findings. This allowed him to mold his profile after the brightest minds shaping the industry's future direction.

Studying the career journeys, capabilities, and personal brands of those already thriving in your desired profession makes your transition goals tangible rather than hypothetical. You understand the full scope of what's needed to be competitive. It illuminates the "hidden curriculum" of skills and experiences that don't show up on traditional job descriptions but are truly valued. This equips you to strategically fill gaps and hone the right combination of expertise to set yourself up for success.

## Legal and Regulatory Information

Certain professions and industries are governed by laws, regulations, certifications, and licensing requirements that are crucial to understanding before embarking on a career transition into those areas. Not understanding the legal and compliance frameworks needed could result in running afoul of requirements or realizing too late that your qualifications don't align with mandatory credentialing.

For example, when Sandra transitioned from nursing into the financial advisory industry, she had to understand the regulatory landscape. The Securities and Exchange Commission, FINRA, as well as state securities divisions each had their own registration standards and compliance obligations for investment advisors. She learned certifications like the Certified Financial Planner (CFP) were considered minimum requirements at many firms.

Her research showed that beyond passing qualification exams, there were strict disclosure rules, documentation standards, constraints around fee structures, and auditing procedures advisors must follow meticulously. Understanding this regulatory maze allowed Sandra to map out the needed exams, approvals, and compliance plans before formally launching her new profession.

Those exploring careers in fields like law, accounting, architecture, engineering and education will find that state-issued licenses are universal gating criteria. In many cases, holding the appropriate license is legally required to practice or receive compensation in that vocation. Researching the specific licensing protocols, required exams, continuing education, and application processes is essential groundwork.

Even roles in fields not traditionally seen as "regulated" may have credentialing protocols to adhere to. Cybersecurity and data privacy have increasing certification schemes like CISSP, CIPP or GIAC around proper handling of information. Human resources roles have certifications like SHRM-CP. Logistics and supply chain jobs have operational standards.

Spending time researching the precise legal and regulatory frameworks of your new target industry provides you with a realistic assessment of necessary credentials upfront. It highlights critical steps requiring significant advanced preparation, testing, documentation, or approval processes. With this regulatory roadmap in hand, you can enter your new field with full confidence you've cleared all the compliance hurdles properly.

## Online Courses and Certifications

Continuously upskilling and acquiring new credentials have become essential for a successful career transition. Fortunately, the rise of online education has made skill development more accessible and affordable than ever before. When vetting potential new vocational paths, explore the vast array of online courses, certifications, and digital credentialing programs available.

Jenna considered pivoting into UX design roles after a marketing career. She compared Coursera, edX, and Udacity course offerings, which featured instruction from MIT, Georgia Tech, and Caltech. Course content ranging from human-computer interaction and interface design to user research methods and wireframing would allow her to build a solid foundational skill base.

Additionally, she found highly-rated courses taught by seasoned UX professionals on platforms like Interaction Design Foundation and Springboard. These industry-trained experts offered specialized curriculums like mobile UX design, UX writing, and strategies for acing portfolio reviews with hiring managers. Their real-world perspectives would prove invaluable.

For certifications, Jenna discovered UX certifications from edX, Google, and Adobe that could boost her credibility with employers. She also explored inexpensive microcredential programs from universities like

Michigan and Wisconsin that delivered sharper skills in areas like voice interface design.

Across all these options, she analyzed factors like pricing, instructor qualifications, workload expectations, capstone projects, and job placement assistance to determine which combinations best aligned with her goals, learning style, budget, and timeline. This comprehensive view of upskilling resources allows for strategically assembling a plan.

Similarly rigorous research can be done for virtually any professional domain - from project management, to data analytics, to coding languages, to trades like electrician or HVAC repair. The digital skills ecosystem provides an incredibly rich landscape of reputable, stackable credential opportunities from prestigious universities, industry leaders, and self-paced programs.

With thoughtful curation of the ideal learning path, you can confidently invest in developing the competencies, credentials, and confidence to demonstrate your qualifications for your next career transition. Online courses make upskilling more affordable and accessible than ever.

Scams and Red Flags

The open nature of the internet has empowered scammers and bad actors to proliferate fraudulent job postings, fake employment offers, and even fictitious companies designed to dupe unsuspecting job seekers. When conducting online research into new careers, it's crucial to maintain a heightened sense of skepticism to avoid falling victim.

Some common red flags to watch out for include job listings with excessive typos or grammatical errors, roles with vague or questionable responsibilities, postings that don't specify the company name, and opportunities promising unrealistic wages or benefits for the work described. If an employer asks for financial information like credit card numbers before interviewing you, that should raise alarms.

Thoroughly vet any unfamiliar company by cross-checking to see if they have an updated, professional website with detailed information on their leadership team, location, clients, or partners. Review Glassdoor and the

Better Business Bureau for any complaints. Be wary if they lack an online presence beyond the job posting itself.

When researching programs that require an upfront payment like some training bootcamps or certification courses do, read reviews and check their accreditation status. Legitimate vocational programs should be able to provide data on graduation rates, career placement stats, and student testimonials. If the outcomes seem too good to be true, they likely are. However, before rejecting a program or school summarily, go online to look for graduates and speak with them about their experience with the program or school.

Even for legitimate-looking opportunities, do not pay for access to job postings or provide sensitive personal details like your Social Security number or immigration status until you've firmly secured and accepted an offer through official channels. Reputable employers and recruiters will never ask for this upfront. A job board might, but an employer or recruiter shouldn't.

Remember, malicious actors prey upon those feeling desperation around securing new employment. Trusting your gut instinct is important – if an email, website, or job post seems suspiciously unprofessional or too brimming with unrealistic promises, steer clear. With cross-verification and due diligence, you can minimize the risk or altogether avoid being cheated.

Effective online research isn't a one-time box to check off, but rather an ongoing process that will help you throughout your entire career transition and beyond. As you begin putting one foot in front of the other down this new vocational path, make a habit of continually gathering fresh insights, revisiting your findings with a critical eye, and adapting your strategies based on the latest information you uncover.

Immersing yourself in industry publications, forums, and thought leader content will keep you tapped into emerging trends, disruptive forces, and evolving best practices. You'll develop a refined understanding of which specific skills and experiences are most highly valued by employers at any given moment. This will help you to pivot your professional development when needed, ensuring you remain competitively positioned.

Your initial online research may have illuminated the landscape, but consistently updating your knowledge will reveal new opportunities you may not have anticipated. You may identify exciting career specializations perfectly aligned to your interests. Or you could discover innovative companies at the cutting edge that represent ideal cultural fits. Maintaining this continuous learning mindset will expand your horizons.

Furthermore, as your experience grows in this new field, you'll gain a sharper lens for discerning trusted, credible sources of information from misleading ones. You'll have real-world context for accurately interpreting job requirements, compensation benchmarks, professional network advice, and more. Your research abilities will elevate in lockstep with your hard-won expertise.

This iterative research process empowers you to make carefully calculated decisions at each stage rather than operating based on assumptions. You'll cultivate a solid foundation of knowledge that allows you to enter your new career trajectory confidently while positioning yourself to navigate future industry evolutions. Consistent online research is an integral tool, not just for informing your transition, but for sustaining long-term career success.

# Step 6:

# Craft a Winning First Impression

When transitioning to a new career, your resume, cover letter, and LinkedIn profile become your primary tools for showcasing your qualifications and convincing potential employers that you're a perfect fit. Tailoring these is crucial.

That's because first impressions are more important than ever, especially for those embarking on a career change. As you try to step into a new career, these serve as your ambassadors, often making that critical first impression before you ever set foot in an interview. They are not merely a list of your past experiences or a formality in the application process; they are powerful marketing tools that can open doors to new opportunities or, if poorly crafted, close them firmly shut.

For career changers, the stakes are even higher. You're not just competing against other people with similar backgrounds; you're often up against individuals who have spent years honing their skills in the industry or field you're trying to enter. This is where the art of tailoring your resume and cover letter becomes not just important, but essential.

Tailoring goes beyond simply adjusting a few words or phrases. It involves a comprehensive reimagining of your professional narrative. It requires you to view your entire work history through the lens of your new career, identifying and highlighting the skills, experiences, and achievements most relevant to your target role. This process demands introspection, research, and a deep understanding of what your potential new employers are looking for.

By customizing them, you're not just presenting your qualifications, you're crafting a compelling argument for why your unique background makes you an ideal hire. You're showing potential employers that despite coming from a different industry or field, you possess transferable skills, adaptability, and, perhaps, a fresh perspective that can bring value to their organization.

Here, I'll explore strategies and techniques that can help you transform your resume, cover letter and LinkedIn profile into powerful tools for career transition. We are going to explore how to present yourself as not just a qualified individual, but as the perfect fit for your new chosen path. Remember, when doing a career transition, a well-crafted resume and cover letter can be the difference between being seen as an outsider and being recognized as the innovative, cross-functional talent that forward-thinking companies are eager to embrace.
Writing Your Resume and LinkedIn Profile

**Relevant Experience:**

When crafting your resume and LinkedIn profile for a career transition, showcase the relevant experience you have. Your goal is to demonstrate that despite coming from a different field or job, you possess valuable skills and experiences that translate well to your target industry and/or career. This process begins with reframing your past roles through the lens of your new career. For each position, highlight responsibilities and achievements that align with your target industry. This might involve creative reinterpretation of your duties, focusing on the aspects that are most applicable to your new field.

Emphasizing transferable skills is crucial to this. Identify skills from your current work that are valuable in your target career or industry, such as project management, leadership, problem-solving, or communication skills. These universal competencies can often bridge the gap between disparate industries, showing potential employers that you have the foundational abilities to be successful for them.

Quantifying your achievements adds credibility to your claims and helps potential employers understand the concrete impact you've had in your previous roles. Use numbers, percentages, and other measurable outcomes to demonstrate the effect of your work, regardless of the industry. This approach not only showcases your ability to drive results but also helps translate your accomplishments into terms that resonate in your new field.

Highlighting relevant projects can be particularly effective when your overall role isn't directly related to your new career. These projects serve as concrete examples of how you've applied skills relevant to your target industry, even if they weren't the primary focus of your previous positions. They can demonstrate your ability to take initiative and your genuine interest in the field you're transitioning into.

Don't overlook the value of volunteer work and side projects in demonstrating relevant experience. Volunteering can be especially powerful for career changers because it often represents your first forays into a new field. They demonstrate initiative, passion, and a willingness to learn, all qualities highly valued by employers considering people who are not square pegs trying to fit a square hole.

Using industry-specific language throughout your resume and LinkedIn profile is a subtle but effective way to show that you understand and can operate in your target field. This involves researching your new industry thoroughly and incorporating relevant terminology into your experience descriptions. It signals to potential employers that you've done your homework and are serious about your career transition and can communicate effectively with others.

Finally, be strategic with the placement of your most relevant experiences. If you have limited directly relevant experience, consider using a functional or combination resume format. This allows you to highlight your most applicable skills and experiences prominently, rather than burying them in a strict reverse chronological order. On LinkedIn, you can use the summary section to immediately draw attention to your most relevant qualifications and your motivation for changing careers.

Remember, the overarching aim is to help potential employers connect the dots between your past experiences and the requirements of your target role. By thoughtfully presenting your relevant experience, you can show that your unique background is not just acceptable, but potentially advantageous in your new career path. This approach transforms your diverse experience from a potential obstacle into a compelling narrative of adaptability, broad perspective, and unique value proposition.

## Transferable Skills

When doing a career transition, transferable skills are your secret weapon. These are the competencies you've honed in your current field that can be effectively applied in your new one. Identifying and showcasing these skills can bridge the gap between your past experiences and future aspirations, demonstrating to potential employers that you're not starting from scratch, but bringing valuable expertise to them.

For example, Maria, a former elementary school teacher successfully transitioned into corporate training. At first glance, these fields might seem worlds apart, but Maria recognized the core skills that united them. Her ability to break down complex concepts into digestible parts, a skill honed through years of teaching young children, became invaluable in creating training modules for adult learners. Her classroom management skills translated seamlessly into facilitating group training sessions and managing diverse personalities in a corporate setting.

Leadership is another highly transferable skill that can manifest in various ways across different careers. James, for instance, was a military veteran who moved into project management in the tech industry. His experience leading teams in high-pressure situations proved invaluable when coordinating complex software development projects with tight deadlines. His ability to motivate team members, make quick decisions, and maintain composure under stress – all skills developed in the military – made him an asset in his new role, despite his initial lack of tech industry experience.

Communication skills are universally valuable and often highly transferable. Sarah, a former journalist, leveraged her interviewing and storytelling abilities to excel in a new career in market research. Her knack for asking probing questions and distilling complex information into clear, concise reports made her effective in her new field. Sarah's experience crafting compelling narratives also proved invaluable in presenting research findings to clients, demonstrating how skills from one field can be creatively applied in another.

Problem-solving is another skill that transcends industry boundaries. Take Alex, a former mechanic who transitioned into IT support. While the specific technical knowledge differed, the underlying approach to diagnosing and resolving issues remained the same. Alex's methodical troubleshooting skills, honed through years of identifying and fixing car problems, translated remarkably well to debugging computer systems and resolving user issues.

Highlighting adaptability can be particularly powerful for career changers. Emily, a former professional athlete, successfully transitioned into corporate sales by emphasizing her ability to quickly learn new skills, perform under pressure, and maintain a goal-oriented mindset. These qualities, cultivated through years of competitive sports, proved highly valuable in the fast-paced, results-driven sales career.

When showcasing transferable skills, it's important to provide concrete examples of how you've applied these skills in your previous roles. Instead of simply listing "project management" as a skill, describe a specific project you managed, the challenges you overcame, and the results you achieved. This approach not only demonstrates that you possess the skill but also shows how you've practically applied it in a professional context. Remember, the key is to help potential employers see the value in your diverse experience. By effectively highlighting your transferable skills, you're showing what you've done and what you're capable of doing in a new context. This narrative can transform you from an outsider to a unique asset, bringing a fresh perspective and a robust skill set to your new chosen field.

**Keyword Optimization**

Keyword optimization has become a critical strategy for career changers trying to break into a new field. This process involves strategically incorporating industry-specific terms, job titles, and relevant phrases throughout your resume and online profiles. The goal is twofold: to pass through Applicant Tracking Systems (ATS) that filter candidates based on keyword matches and to resonate with hiring managers who are looking for specific skills and experiences.
Take the case of David, a former retail manager transitioning into human

resources. Initially, his resume was filled with retail-specific jargon that didn't align with HR terminology. After researching his target industry, he revamped his resume, replacing phrases like "sales targets" and "inventory management" with HR-centric terms such as "talent acquisition," "employee relations," and "performance management." This simple yet effective change resulted in his resume being shortlisted for several HR positions, opening doors that were previously closed.

Another example is Lisa, a teacher moving into the tech industry as a UX designer. She realized that her educational terminology wasn't resonating with technical recruiters. By integrating phrases like "user-centered design," "wireframing," and "usability testing" into her resume, and relating her teaching experiences to these concepts, Lisa was able to showcase her relevant skills in a language that tech companies understood. This keyword optimization led to a significant increase in responses to her job applications.

The story of Michael, a journalist transitioning into content marketing, highlights the importance of job title alignment. Instead of listing his previous role as "Reporter," he opted for "Content Creator," which more closely matched the positions he was applying for. He also peppered his resume with marketing-specific terms like "SEO," "conversion rates," and "content strategy." This approach not only helped his resume pass through ATS filters but also immediately signaled to hiring managers that he understood the key concepts of content marketing.

However, it's crucial to strike a balance between keyword optimization and maintaining readability. Sarah, a finance professional moving into sustainability consulting, initially overloaded her resume with every sustainability-related term she could find. The result was a document that felt forced and unnatural. She refined her approach, focusing on integrating key phrases like "environmental impact assessment," "sustainable development," and "corporate social responsibility" in a way that flowed naturally with her experiences. This balanced approach resulted in a resume that was both ATS-friendly and engaging for human readers.

For career changers, industry certifications and training programs can be goldmines for relevant keywords. When Alex, a former chef, decided to pursue a career in project management, he completed a Project Management Professional (PMP) certification. By prominently featuring this certification and incorporating terms like "Agile methodology," "risk management," and "stakeholder communication" into his resume, he effectively signaled his commitment to and understanding of his new field. LinkedIn profiles offer another opportunity for keyword optimization. Emma, transitioning from marketing to data analysis, revamped her LinkedIn headline and summary to include phrases like "data visualization," "statistical analysis," and "predictive modeling." She also joined relevant LinkedIn groups and participated in discussions, learning how to naturally incorporate industry terms into her posts and comments. Doing this not only optimized her profile for searches but also demonstrated her engagement with the data science community.

Remember, the key to successful keyword optimization is research and authenticity. Spend time studying job descriptions in your target field, industry publications, and the websites of companies you're interested in. Identify the terms and phrases that consistently appear, and thoughtfully incorporate them into your resume and online profiles. However, ensure that you can speak to these terms in an interview setting – keyword optimization should reflect your genuine skills and experiences, not create a false representation of your capabilities.

By mastering the art of keyword optimization, you can significantly increase your visibility to potential employers, effectively bridging the gap between your past experiences and your future career aspirations.

## Quantify Achievements

In the landscape of career transitions, the ability to quantify your achievements serves as a powerful tool to bridge the gap between your past experiences and future aspirations. By translating your accomplishments into concrete numbers, percentages, and metrics, you provide potential employers with tangible evidence of your capabilities, regardless of the industry you're coming from.

Rachel was a teacher transitioning into corporate training. Initially, her resume simply stated that she "improved student performance." However, when she revised this to "Increased average test scores by 27% over one academic year by implementing personalized learning strategies," her applications started garnering much more attention. This specific, quantified achievement demonstrated not just her teaching ability, but also her capacity to drive measurable results - a skill highly valued in the corporate world.

James, a retail manager moving into operations management, faced the challenge of making his retail experience relevant to his target industry. Rather than simply stating he "managed a successful store," he quantified his achievements: "Increased store revenue by 35% year-over-year while reducing operational costs by 15% by implementing lean management principles." This approach not only showcased his impact but also demonstrated his understanding of key business metrics that translate across industries.

The power of quantifying your impact is not limited to financial metrics. When Sarah, a nonprofit coordinator, decided to transition into project management in the tech sector, she struggled to make her experience seem relevant. By quantifying her achievements - "Coordinated 50+ volunteers to execute 6 community projects annually, consistently meeting project deadlines while 20% under budget" - she was able to demonstrate her project management skills in a way that resonated with tech companies.

Even soft skills can be quantified for greater impact. Alex was a customer service representative who wanted to transition into human resources. Instead of simply listing "strong communication skills," he quantified his achievement: "Maintained a 98% customer satisfaction rating over 3 years, handling an average of 100 customer interactions daily." This not only proved his communication prowess but also his consistency and ability to perform under pressure.

For career changers coming from fields where quantifying your impact might seem challenging, creative approaches can be effective. Lisa, an artist transitioning into marketing, quantified her achievements by stating, "Created and managed social media content that grew follower base by 500% in 6 months, leading to 3 commissioned projects valued at $15,000." This not only showcased her social media marketing skills but also demonstrated her ability to translate online engagement into tangible business results.

The impact of quantification extends beyond the resume. During interviews, these specific achievements provide talking points that allow you to tell compelling stories about your experiences. Mark, a former journalist moving into public relations, used his quantified achievements - "Increased readership by 40% through implementation of data-driven content strategies" - as a springboard to discuss his approach to audience engagement, a skill highly relevant in PR.

However, it's crucial to strike a balance. Shamika, in her transition from sales to marketing, initially filled her resume with so many numbers that it became overwhelming. She learned to focus on the most impactful metrics, using them to tell a coherent story of her career progression and achievements.

Remember, the goal of quantifying achievements is not just to impress with numbers, but to provide concrete evidence of your impact and potential. When transitioning careers, these quantified achievements can serve as a universal language, allowing hiring managers to understand your capabilities in terms relevant to their industry.

By mastering the art of quantifying your achievements, you transform your resume from a list of past job duties into a powerful testament to your ability to drive results. This approach not only helps you stand out in a sea of career changers but also gives potential employers the confidence that your unique background brings measurable value to their organization.

**Education and Certifications**

When trying to transition careers, education and certifications can serve as powerful bridges, connecting your past experiences to your future aspirations. These credentials not only demonstrate your commitment to your new field but also provide tangible evidence of your relevant knowledge and skills.

Michael was an elementary school teacher who decided to pivot into the data science. Recognizing the knowledge gap, Michael enrolled in an online Data Science bootcamp. Upon completion, he proudly listed this certification on his resume, alongside specific projects he had completed during the course. This addition to his profile caught the eye of a hiring manager at a tech startup, who was impressed by his initiative and newly acquired skills. During interviews, Michael was able to discuss how he applied his teaching background to break down complex data concepts, combining his new technical knowledge with his innate ability to explain difficult ideas simply.

Similarly, consider the case of Star, a marketing professional transitioning into environmental sustainability. Her bachelor's degree in marketing seemed unrelated to her new career path at first glance. However, she supplemented her existing education with a certification in Sustainable Business Practices from a recognized online platform. This additional credential not only showcased her commitment to her new field but also provided her with industry-specific knowledge that she could immediately apply. In her cover letter, she was able to draw parallels between her marketing expertise and her newfound understanding of sustainability, presenting herself as a unique candidate who could effectively communicate complex environmental issues to diverse audiences.

The power of relevant coursework should not be underestimated, even if it doesn't result in a full degree or certification. Glenn, a former retail manager aspiring to enter human resources, didn't have the time or resources for a full HR degree. Instead, he completed several online courses in topics like Employment Law, Talent Acquisition, and Performance Management. By listing these courses on his resume and discussing the key concepts he learned in his cover letter, James was able to demonstrate his dedication to HR and his understanding of core principles, despite his non-traditional background.

Certifications can be particularly impactful for career changers. Markie, transitioning from journalism to project management, obtained a Project Management Professional (PMP) certification. This internationally recognized credential immediately signaled to potential employers that she possessed a standardized set of project management skills, despite coming from a different industry. During interviews, Emma could confidently discuss project management methodologies and best practices, bridging the gap between her past experiences in coordinating news stories and her potential to manage complex business projects.

For some, pursuing a complete career change might involve returning to formal education. This was the case for Alex, a former chef who decided to become a software developer, enrolled in a Computer Science degree program, balancing part-time studies with his existing job. Even before completing his degree, she was able to list her ongoing education on her resume, along with relevant coursework and coding projects. This demonstrated to potential employers not only her growing technical skills but also her dedication and ability to manage multiple commitments effectively.

It's important to note that education and certifications don't always have to be directly related to your new field to be valuable. Lisa, moving from accounting to marketing, highlighted a public speaking course she had taken. While not specifically a marketing certification, this course demonstrated her commitment to improving her communication skills - a vital asset in marketing. During interviews, Lisa was able to discuss how this course prepared her to present marketing strategies confidently to clients and stakeholders.

Remember, when highlighting education and certifications in your career transition journey, it's not just about listing credentials. It's about weaving a narrative that connects your past, your new knowledge, and your future aspirations. Explain how each educational experience has prepared you for your new career, and be ready to discuss specific skills or knowledge you've gained that are relevant to your target role.

By strategically showcasing your education and certifications, you can demonstrate not only your qualifications but also your adaptability, your commitment to growth, and your ability to acquire new skills - all highly valuable traits in today's rapidly evolving job market. This approach transforms your educational background from a potential obstacle into a compelling story of personal and professional development, making you a unique and attractive candidate in your new chosen field.

# Professional Summary or Branding Statement

When you are changing careers, a well-crafted professional summary or branding statement acts as a powerful introduction, setting the stage for your unique narrative. This concise yet impactful pitch encapsulates your strengths, skills, and the distinctive value you bring to your new career path, serving as a bridge between your past experiences and future aspirations.

For example, Sonia, a former high school English teacher was transitioning into corporate communications. Initially, her resume opened with a bland objective statement about seeking a position in communications. After revising her approach, she crafted a compelling branding statement: "Dynamic communicator with 10 years of experience distilling complex ideas into engaging narratives. Combining pedagogical expertise with a passion for clear, impactful messaging to drive organizational success." This powerful opening immediately reframed her teaching background as an asset in corporate communications, catching the eye of a hiring manager at a firm who was looking for someone who could explain their products in simple, relatable terms.

Anthony, a veteran transitioning from military service to project management, faced the challenge of translating his experience into civilian terms. His branding statement effectively bridged this gap: "Results-driven leader with a proven track record of executing complex, high-stakes projects in challenging environments. Leveraging military precision and adaptability to drive project success in the corporate world." This statement not only highlighted Anthony's transferable skills but also positioned his unique background as an advantage. During an interview, a hiring manager specifically mentioned being intrigued by how his military experience could bring a fresh perspective to their project management approach.

For career changers, addressing the transition head-on in the branding statement can be powerful. Erica wanted to move from finance to environmental sustainability. Her summary read: "Financial analyst turned sustainability advocate, combining data-driven decision-making with a passion for environmental stewardship. Leveraging 8 years of experience in financial modeling to drive sustainable business practices and bottom-line growth." This approach acknowledged her career shift while emphasizing how her financial background could be an asset in her new field. It led to an interview where she was able to discuss how her financial acumen could help companies see sustainability not just as an ethical choice, but as a sound business decision.

A branding statement can also be an opportunity to showcase your commitment to your new field. Richard, transitioning from retail management to UX design, used his statement to highlight both his relevant skills and his dedication to his new career: "Customer-centric professional with 5+ years in retail management, now applying human-centered design principles to create intuitive digital experiences. Combining hands-on customer insight with newly acquired UX design skills to bridge the gap between user needs and business goals." This statement not only highlighted his relevant experience but also signaled his proactive approach to acquiring new skills, which resonated with employers looking for adaptable, self-motivated candidates.

For those making a significant career leap, the branding statement can help connect seemingly disparate experiences. Kate, a former professional athlete moving into corporate sales, crafted a statement that drew powerful parallels: "Elite athlete turned sales professional, bringing the same dedication, competitive drive, and team-oriented mindset that led to Olympic success into the corporate arena. Transforming the pursuit of athletic excellence into a passion for exceeding sales targets and driving business growth." This unique angle caught the attention of a sales director who saw the potential in her athletic mindset and invited her for an interview, despite her lack of traditional sales experience.

Remember, the key to an effective branding statement or professional summary is authenticity combined with strategic positioning. It should feel true to who you are while also speaking directly to the needs of your target industry. Maria, transitioning from social work to human resources, struck this balance perfectly: "Empathetic people-person with a background in social work, now leveraging a deep understanding of human behavior and conflict resolution to foster positive workplace cultures and drive employee engagement." This statement effectively reframed her social work experience as relevant and valuable in an HR context, leading to several interview opportunities where she could expand on how her unique background prepared her for HR challenges.

Crafting an impactful branding statement or professional summary is an iterative process. It requires deep reflection on your skills, experiences, and the unique value you bring, combined with a clear understanding of what your target industry needs. When done well, it serves as a powerful opening statement in your career transition story, compelling hiring managers to read on and discover the full potential you offer in your newly chosen field.

For Your Cover Letter:

## Customization

A meticulously customized cover letter can be the key that unlocks new opportunities. Far from being a mere formality, a well-crafted, personalized cover letter demonstrates your real interest in the position and your understanding of the company's unique needs.

Consider the case of Olivia, a former librarian aspiring to enter the field of data analytics. For each application, Olivia diligently researched the company and the specific role. When applying to a healthcare analytics firm, she opened her cover letter with, "Dear Dr. Thompson, I am writing to express my strong interest in the Data Analyst position (Job ID: DA2024) at HealthMetrics Inc." This immediate personalization and specificity caught Dr. Thompson's attention, prompting him to read on with heightened interest.

Olivia didn't stop there. She went on to reference a recent article about HealthMetrics' innovative approach to patient data management, linking it to her own experience organizing and analyzing large datasets in her library work. This level of customization not only showcased Olivia's research skills but also demonstrated how her unique background could add value to HealthMetrics' mission.

The power of personalization was equally evident in the case of Rahul, a former sous chef looking to break into event management. When applying to a boutique event planning company, Rahul addressed his cover letter to "Ms. Angela Chen, Head of Talent Acquisition," whom he had identified through LinkedIn research. He opened with, "Your recent event for the City Museum's annual gala, which seamlessly blended culinary artistry with immersive storytelling, inspired me to apply for the Event Coordinator position at your firm."

This opening not only showed Rahul's familiarity with the company's work but also subtly hinted at how his culinary background could be an asset in creating unique event experiences. Ms. Chen later mentioned that this personalized opening was what prompted her to invite Rahul for an interview, despite his non-traditional background.

The impact of customization extends beyond just the opening paragraph. Tanya, transitioning from teaching to corporate training, tailored each paragraph of her cover letter to address specific requirements mentioned in the job description for a Learning and Development Specialist at a company. She wrote, "Your emphasis on creating engaging, multimedia training content aligns perfectly with my experience developing interactive lesson plans and educational videos that increased student engagement by 40%."

By directly addressing the company's stated needs and linking them to her relevant experiences, Tanya effectively reframed her teaching background as valuable experience for corporate training. The hiring manager was impressed by how Tanya's cover letter seemed to speak directly to their needs, leading to an invitation for an interview.

Sometimes, customization can involve acknowledging and addressing potential concerns. When Lucas, a former professional musician, applied for a project management role at a construction firm, he knew his background might seem incongruous. In his cover letter, he wrote, "While my background in professional music might seem an unusual fit for construction project management, my experience coordinating complex musical productions, managing diverse teams of artists and technicians, and delivering performances on time and on budget has equipped me with skills directly applicable to your field."

This proactive approach to addressing his unconventional background, coupled with the personalized opening and specific references to current projects, intrigued Mr. Rodriguez enough to schedule an interview with Lucas.

The art of customization also extends to adapting your tone and style to match the company culture. When Amelia, a former corporate lawyer, applied for a creative director position at a hip advertising agency, she departed from her usual formal tone. Her opening to Zoe Chang, Creative VP at the firm, read, "Your recent campaign for xxxx blew my mind and got me thinking – what if we could bring that same level of creative disruption to legal and financial services marketing?"

This more casual, enthusiastic tone matched the firm's brand voice and immediately positioned Amelia as someone who understood and could adapt to their culture. Zoe later commented that Amelia's cover letter stood out for its perfect blend of professional experience and creative energy.

In each of these cases, the job seekers went beyond simply changing a few names and details. They invested time in understanding the company, the role, and the person they were addressing. They crafted each cover letter as a unique piece of communication, designed to resonate with its specific reader.

Remember, in the competitive landscape of career transitions, a customized cover letter is your opportunity to tell your story in a way that directly addresses the company's needs. It's your chance to show not just that you want any job, but that you want this job, at this company. This level of personalization can be the differentiator that moves your application from the stack to the "must interview" pile.

## Explaining the Transition

When making a career transition, addressing the shift head-on in your cover letter can transform a potential obstacle into a compelling narrative. Your explanation will not only provide context for your interest in the role but also demonstrate self-awareness, adaptability, and commitment to your new chosen path.

Priya was a former accountant venturing into sustainable fashion design. In her cover letter to one firm, she wrote, "After a decade of analyzing numbers, I've decided to pursue my lifelong passion for sustainable fashion. This transition isn't just a career change; it's a commitment to combining my analytical skills with my creative vision to drive positive change in the fashion industry." Priya then went on to detail the fashion design courses she had completed and the sustainable materials workshop she had attended, showcasing her proactive approach to learning relevant skills.

The hiring manager was intrigued by her unique background, seeing potential in how her financial acumen could contribute to creating both eco-friendly and economically viable designs. This led to an interview where Priya could elaborate on how her diverse skill set could benefit the company.

For some, the career transition is driven by a desire to make a broader impact. This was the case for Dmitri, a software engineer moving into renewable energy project management. In his cover letter to one firm he explained, "While I've enjoyed solving complex coding challenges, I've realized my true calling lies in tackling the global climate crisis. I'm eager to apply my technical problem-solving skills to managing renewable energy projects that can make a tangible difference in our world." Dmitri then highlighted the online courses in renewable energy technologies and project management he had completed to prepare for this transition.

The Director of Operations at the firm was impressed by Dmitri's clear explanation of his motivations and initiative in acquiring relevant knowledge. This explanation turned what could have been seen as a lack of direct experience into a story of passion and dedication, leading to an invitation for an in-person interview.

Sometimes, life events can spark a career transition. This was true for Naomi, a former emergency room nurse transitioning into health tech product management. In her cover letter to one company, she wrote, "After witnessing firsthand the challenges healthcare professionals face with outdated technology, I've been inspired to bridge the gap between medical expertise and technological innovation. My transition into health tech product management is driven by a desire to create solutions that streamline patient care and improve health outcomes." She then detailed the product management certification she had earned and the health tech hackathon she had participated in, demonstrating her commitment to her new career path.

The CEO was particularly moved by Naomi's connection to the field and saw great value in her firsthand understanding of healthcare professionals' needs. This led to a series of interviews where Naomi could showcase how her unique background could inform user-centric product development.

For some career changers, the transition is about finding new applications for existing skills. This was the case for Marcus, a former professional basketball player moving into corporate team building and leadership development. In his cover letter to one company, he explained, "My years on the court have taught me invaluable lessons about teamwork, leadership, and performing under pressure. Now, I'm excited to bring these insights into the corporate world, helping teams achieve peak performance just as I did in professional sports." Marcus then highlighted the coaching certification he had obtained and the leadership workshops he had conducted for youth organizations, showing how he had already begun applying his sports experience in professional development contexts.

The director of HR was intrigued by his unique perspective on teamwork and leadership. This explanation helped reframe his sports career as highly relevant experience for corporate team building, leading to an invitation for a practical assessment where Marcus could demonstrate his approach. In each of these cases, the career changers used cover letters to address their transitions openly and positively. They didn't shy away from their change in direction but instead framed it as a thoughtful, motivated decision. By explaining their motivations and detailing the steps they had taken to prepare for their new careers, they transformed potential skepticism into interest in their unique perspectives and dedicated approach.

Remember, explaining your career transition in your cover letter is an opportunity to show potential employers your self-awareness, your ability to adapt and grow, and your genuine enthusiasm for your newly chosen field. It's a chance to turn your diverse background into a compelling story of personal and professional evolution, positioning yourself as a unique and valuable candidate in your new industry.

## Relevance

Establishing relevance in your cover letter is about creating a narrative that bridges your past experiences with the requirements of your target role, highlighting the transferable skills that make you a valuable candidate despite your non-traditional background.

Elodie, a former ballet dancer, decided to pivot her career towards financial advising. In her cover letter to a boutique wealth management firm, she wrote:

"My 15-year career in professional ballet has instilled in me skills and perspectives that are surprisingly relevant to financial advising. The discipline, precision, and long-term planning required in dance mirror the approach needed for sound financial management."

Elodie then drew specific parallels between her dance experience and financial advising:

"As a principal dancer, I was responsible not just for my performances, but for mentoring younger dancers and contributing to the company's strategic decisions. This experience in leadership and long-term planning aligns well with the role of a financial advisor guiding clients towards their future goals."

She highlighted transferable skills:

"The world of professional dance taught me to manage resources efficiently, both in terms of physical energy and financial constraints. I've navigated the uncertainties of a performance career, learning to budget, invest in myself, and plan for the future - experiences that have given me a unique perspective on financial resilience."

Elodie also emphasized her ability to communicate complex ideas:

"In ballet, we tell intricate stories without words, translating abstract concepts into accessible, emotional experiences. This skill in clear, impactful communication will be invaluable in explaining complex financial concepts to clients from diverse backgrounds."

She concluded by mentioning the steps she had taken to prepare for this career shift:

"To build on my practical experience with financial management, I've completed the Certified Financial Planner (CFP) coursework and passed the exam. I've also been volunteering with a local nonprofit, providing basic financial literacy education to young artists."

The hiring manager was intrigued by her unconventional background. Her unique perspective on financial planning, combined with her formal training and clear communication skills, led to an invitation for an interview. They were particularly interested in how her experiences could help them better serve clients in creative industries.

This story demonstrates how Elodie's background in ballet could be relevantly applied to financial advising, showcasing the unexpected ways in which skills and experiences can transfer across very different fields.

For some, relevance lies in unexpected parallels between industries. This was true for Tarek, a former sommelier venturing into pharmaceutical sales. In his cover letter to one firm, he explained, "My experience in wine sales has equipped me with a deep understanding of how to present complex information in an engaging, accessible manner. Just as I've guided customers through the nuances of wine varieties and food pairings, I'm eager to help healthcare professionals navigate the intricacies of your innovative medications." Tarek then highlighted his track record of exceeding sales targets and building long-term client relationships in the competitive wine industry.

The sales director was impressed by Tarek's ability to draw these connections. His unique background, combined with his clear communication skills, led to an invitation for a sales pitch simulation where Tarek could demonstrate how his wine expertise translated to pharmaceutical sales.

Sometimes, relevance comes from broader life experiences. This was the case for Yuki, a former international aid worker transitioning into corporate social responsibility (CSR). In her cover letter, she wrote, "My years coordinating relief efforts in diverse cultural contexts have given me a firsthand understanding of global social issues and the impact of corporate actions on communities. This experience, combined with my ability to manage complex stakeholder relationships, positions me uniquely to drive meaningful CSR initiatives for your firm." Yuki then detailed specific projects she had managed, emphasizing skills like cross-cultural communication, resource allocation, and impact assessment.

The CSR director was particularly interested in Yuki's global perspective and hands-on experience with social impact projects. This led to a series of interviews where Yuki could share her insights on how this company could enhance its CSR efforts.

For some career changers, relevance is about reframing existing skills in a new context. This was true for Omar, a former criminal defense lawyer moving into cybersecurity policy. In his cover letter, he explained, "My legal career has been centered on protecting individuals' rights and navigating complex regulatory frameworks. In the realm of cybersecurity, I see a parallel challenge: safeguarding digital rights and helping organizations navigate the intricate landscape of data protection laws." Omar then highlighted his experience in research, critical analysis, and presenting complex arguments - all skills directly applicable to developing cybersecurity policies.

The policy director at SecureNet was intrigued by Omar's legal perspective on cybersecurity challenges. His ability to draw clear connections between legal practice and cybersecurity policy led to an in-depth discussion about emerging digital privacy issues.

In each of these cases, the career changers didn't just list their past experiences; they actively interpreted them through the lens of their target roles. They demonstrated not only their relevant skills but also their ability to think creatively about how their unique backgrounds could add value in new contexts.

Remember, establishing relevance in your cover letter is about more than matching keywords from the job description. It's about telling a compelling story of how your diverse experiences have prepared you for this new role in ways that traditional candidates might not match. By thoughtfully connecting your past to the present opportunity, you can transform perceived gaps in your resume into unique strengths, positioning yourself as a candidate who brings fresh perspectives and versatile skills to the table.

Why You're a Fit

Explaining why you're an ideal fit for a company and role is crucial in a cover letter, especially when transitioning careers. Doing this allows you to connect your unique background to the specific needs of the organization, demonstrating not just your qualifications, but also your potential to bring fresh perspectives and innovative solutions.

Begin by thoroughly researching the company's culture, values, and current challenges. Look for areas where your diverse experience can offer unique insights or approaches. Perhaps your background gives you a different perspective on their target market, or your varied skill set allows you to bridge gaps between departments.

Highlight how your non-traditional career path has equipped you with adaptability and breadth of knowledge that can be invaluable in today's rapidly changing business landscape. Emphasize your ability to think creatively, draw connections between disparate fields, and approach problems from multiple angles.

Discuss how your transition itself demonstrates qualities the company might value, such as courage, self-motivation, and a commitment to continuous learning. Your willingness to step out of your comfort zone and acquire new skills shows an adaptability that can be highly attractive to employers.

If the company is facing specific challenges or changes, explain how your background uniquely positions you to help navigate these situations. Perhaps your experience in a different industry offers solutions not yet

considered, or your diverse skill set makes you particularly suited to help with an upcoming project or initiative
.

Don't shy away from addressing how your unconventional background might initially seem like a mismatch. Instead, reframe it as an opportunity for the company to bring in fresh ideas and new approaches. Explain how your unique combination of skills and experiences can help the company innovate, expand into new markets, or improve existing processes.

Remember to align your strengths with the company's mission and values. Show how your personal motivations and professional goals align with those of the organization, demonstrating that you're not just looking for any job, but are specifically drawn to this role and this company.

Ultimately, this section of your cover letter should leave the reader with a clear understanding of not just why you want the job, but why your unique background makes you an exceptionally valuable candidate. It's your opportunity to show that your career transition is not a liability, but a strength that sets you apart from other applicants and offers tangible benefits to the company.

## Show Passion

Demonstrating genuine enthusiasm for your new career path and the specific role you're applying for is a powerful way to captivate potential employers. This passion not only highlights your commitment to the field but also indicates your potential for long-term engagement and growth within the company.

Begin by explaining what drew you to this new career. Discuss the moment of realization or the series of experiences that led you to this transition. This personal narrative can help employers understand your motivation and see your career change as a thoughtful, purposeful decision rather than a random shift.

Delve into the aspects of the new field that genuinely excite you. Whether it's the opportunity to solve complex problems, the chance to make a positive impact, or the thrill of working with cutting-edge technology, conveying your enthusiasm can be infectious. Employers are often drawn to candidates who show a deep interest in the work itself, not just the job title or company name.

Connect your passion to the company's mission and values. Research their recent projects, initiatives, or innovations that align with your interests. Discuss how these elements resonate with your personal and professional goals, showing that your enthusiasm extends beyond the role to the organization as a whole.

Highlight how your unique background fuels your passion for this new direction. Perhaps your previous experiences have given you insights that make you particularly excited about the possibilities in this new field. Explain how this combination of fresh perspective and genuine interest can bring energy and innovation to the role.

Discuss specific aspects of the job description that excite you. Whether it's the opportunity to collaborate with diverse teams, the challenge of meeting ambitious goals, or the chance to learn and apply new skills, showing enthusiasm for the day-to-day responsibilities of the role can set you apart from candidates who might see these as mere tasks to be completed.

Demonstrate how your passion translates into proactive preparation. Discuss any relevant courses, workshops, or self-directed learning you've undertaken in pursuit of this new career. This shows not only enthusiasm but also dedication and a willingness to invest in your own growth.

Convey how your excitement for the role fuels your desire to contribute to the company's success. Explain how your passion drives you to go above and beyond, to seek innovative solutions, and to continuously improve your skills and knowledge.

Remember to balance passion with professionalism. While enthusiasm is valuable, it should be coupled with a clear understanding of the industry, the role, and how you can contribute effectively.

By effectively showcasing your passion, you're not just telling an employer why you want the job; you're showing them the energy, commitment, and drive you'll bring to the role. This enthusiasm, combined with your unique background, can position you as a candidate who offers not just skills and experience, but also the potential to become a dynamic, engaged member of their team.

## Examples and Evidence

Providing concrete examples and evidence of your capabilities demonstrates your skills and achievements that can bridge the gap between your past experiences and your new career aspirations.

Kai was a former professional athlete transitioning into corporate leadership with a small business. In his cover letter, he wrote: "As team captain, I led our squad to three national championships in five years. This experience honed my leadership skills, particularly in motivating diverse personalities towards a common goal. In our championship season, I implemented a peer mentoring system that reduced rookie errors by 30% and improved team cohesion scores by 25%."

This example not only showcased Kai's leadership abilities but also provided quantifiable results that demonstrated his effectiveness. It helped potential employers see how his sports leadership could translate into a corporate setting.

Another powerful approach is to highlight projects or initiatives that align with your new career path. Take the case of Amara, a teacher transitioning into corporate training and development. She wrote: "In my final year of teaching, I developed and implemented a project-based learning curriculum that increased student engagement by 40% and improved standardized test scores by an average of 15%. This experience in curriculum design and performance improvement directly aligns with your company's need for innovative training programs."

Amara's example demonstrates her ability to create effective learning experiences and measure their impact, skills highly valued in corporate training roles.

Sometimes, the most compelling evidence comes from overcoming challenges. Consider Leon, a former small business owner moving into supply chain management. He shared: "When faced with a 200% increase in shipping costs due to global disruptions, I redesigned our entire logistics process. By negotiating with local suppliers and optimizing delivery routes, I reduced shipping costs by 30% and improved delivery times by 25%, all while maintaining product quality."

This example showcases Leon's problem-solving skills, adaptability, and ability to optimize complex processes - all crucial in supply chain management.

For career changers, volunteer work or side projects can provide valuable evidence of skills. Nadia, transitioning from marketing to environmental science, highlighted her volunteer work: "While working in marketing, I led a pro-bono campaign for a local conservation group. Our social media strategy increased community engagement by 150% and helped secure a $500,000 grant for wetland restoration. This project not only honed my data analysis and communication skills but also deepened my commitment to environmental causes."

This example demonstrates Nadia's ability to apply her marketing skills to environmental causes, while also showing her passion and commitment to her new field.

Certifications and additional training can also serve as powerful evidence. Jamal, moving from customer service to cybersecurity, wrote: "To prepare for this career transition, I completed a rigorous cybersecurity bootcamp and earned my CompTIA Security+ certification. During the bootcamp, I led a team project that developed a comprehensive security protocol for a simulated healthcare provider, identifying and addressing 15 critical vulnerabilities."

This example shows Jamal's proactive approach to gaining relevant skills and his ability to apply them in practical scenarios.

Remember, the key is to select examples that demonstrate how your past experiences have equipped you with skills relevant to your new career. By providing specific, quantifiable achievements and connecting them directly to the requirements of your target role, you can paint a vivid picture of your potential value in your new field.

## Seal the Deal: Your Confident Closing

A powerful closing paragraph to your cover letter is vital for leaving a lasting impression and propelling your application forward. This final section should exude confidence, reiterate your enthusiasm, and prompt action.

Consider Zara, transitioning from journalism to public relations. Her closing paragraph read:

"I'm excited about bringing my investigative skills and storytelling expertise to (fill in the company name). I'd welcome the opportunity to discuss how my unique background can contribute to your team's success. I'll follow up next Tuesday to ensure you've received my application and to answer any questions you might have. Feel free to contact me before then if that works better for you. Thank you for your consideration."

Zara's closing is confident, proactive, and specific, setting clear expectations for follow-up.

Miguel, moving from software development to sustainable energy project management, concluded his letter with:

"I'm eager to explore how my technical background and passion for sustainability can drive innovation at (fill in the blank company name). I look forward to the opportunity to discuss this exciting role further. I'll touch base early next week to confirm receipt of my application. Thank you for your time and consideration."

Miguel's closing reiterates his unique value proposition while expressing genuine enthusiasm for the role.

Aisha, transitioning from teaching to corporate training, ended her letter on a strong note:

"I'm thrilled at the prospect of applying my classroom management and curriculum development skills to elevate (fill in the blank company name)'s training programs. I'd love to meet with you to elaborate upon how my experience can benefit your team. I'll follow up this Friday to ensure my application has been received. Thank you for considering my application." Aisha's closing confidently connects her past experience to the new role while setting a clear timeline for follow-up.

Remember, a strong closing should:

1. Reiterate your enthusiasm for the role and company
2. Express confidence in your ability to contribute
3. Request an interview or further discussion
4. Indicate a specific time for follow-up
5. Thank the reader for their time and consideration

By ending your cover letter with confidence and clarity, you leave the reader with a strong final impression and a clear next step, increasing the likelihood of a positive response to your application.

Striking the Right Chord: Professional Eloquence

Maintaining a professional and positive tone in your cover letter is crucial for making a strong impression. This balance of professionalism and enthusiasm can significantly impact how your application is received.

According to a 2020 study by TopResume, 48% of hiring managers say they're more likely to pay attention to a cover letter that's tailored to their open position [1]. This underscores the importance of not just what you say, but how you say it.

Consider Elena's approach when transitioning from hospitality management to healthcare administration:

"I'm excited to bring my decade of experience in customer satisfaction and operational efficiency to (hospital name). My background in managing diverse teams and streamlining processes aligns well with your commitment to patient-centered care and operational excellence."

Elena's tone is professional yet enthusiastic, succinctly highlighting her relevant skills.

Raj, moving from finance to nonprofit management, struck a similar balance:

"I'm eager to apply my financial acumen to advance (non-profit's name)'s mission. My experience with budget optimization and strategic planning could help maximize the impact of your valuable donor contributions."

Raj's tone conveys both his expertise and passion for the organization's mission.

Research by CareerBuilder found that 77% of employers consider cover letters to be important, with many using them to evaluate a person's writing skills [2]. This highlights the need for clear, concise communication.

Keep your cover letter focused and brief. Aim for 3-4 paragraphs that pack a punch. Any longer, and you risk losing the reader's attention.

Key elements of a professional tone include:

1. Confidence without arrogance
2. Enthusiasm tempered with realism
3. Formality balanced with approachability
4. Conciseness without sacrificing clarity

Remember, your cover letter is often your first impression. A professional tone showcases your communication skills and demonstrates your understanding of workplace etiquette, both valuable assets in any career transition.

1. TopResume. (2020). "Job Search Statistics: 2020 Job Search & Hiring Trends"
2. CareerBuilder. (2019). "Annual Job Seeker Survey"

Remember that both your resume and cover letter are living documents. Tailor them for each application, addressing the specific requirements and culture of the company you're applying to. Careful tailoring increases your chances of progressing to the interview stage.

This principle of customization is crucial in today's competitive job market, especially for those navigating career transitions. Your resume and cover letter should evolve with each application, reflecting not just your skills and experiences, but also your understanding of each unique opportunity.

When tailoring resumes and cover letters, always do the following:

1. **Job Description Analysis:** Carefully review the job posting, identifying key skills, qualifications, and responsibilities. Demonstrate these in your documents, using similar or preferably identical language where appropriate.

2. **Company Research:** Investigate the company's mission, values, recent projects, and culture. Incorporate this knowledge into your application to demonstrate genuine interest and cultural fit.

3. **Industry-Specific Language:** Adapt your vocabulary to match industry-specific terms and jargon, showcasing your familiarity with the field.

4. **Highlighting Relevant Experiences:** Emphasize experiences and skills most pertinent to the specific role, even if they weren't the primary focus of your previous positions.

5. **Addressing Company Needs:** Frame your skills and experiences in terms of how they can address the company's current challenges or contribute to their goals.

6. **Quantifiable Achievements:** Where possible, include measurable accomplishments that relate to the target role's key performance indicators.

7. **Tone and Style:** Adjust the tone of your documents to match the company culture – more formal for traditional industries, potentially more casual for startups or creative fields.

8. **Length and Format:** Tailor the length and format of your documents to industry standards and company preferences.

9. **Addressing Gaps:** If you're changing careers, directly address how your background prepares you for this new direction.

10. **Future-Oriented Statements:** Include forward-looking statements that show how you plan to grow and contribute in the new role.

This process requires time and effort for each application, but it significantly increases your chances of making a strong impression and being interviewed if qualified. It demonstrates your serious interest in the position and your ability to understand and meet their specific needs.

Moreover, this customization process helps you refine your career narrative. With each tailored application, you'll gain a clearer understanding of how your unique background fits into your newly chosen field.

Remember, in a career transition, your goal is not just to show that you can do the job, but that your diverse experiences make you an exceptionally valuable new hire. By carefully tailoring your resume and cover letter, you transform these documents from mere summaries of your past into powerful arguments for your future potential.

Step 7:

# Mastering Your New Path: The Power of Continuous Learning

In today's economy, the adage "knowledge is power" has never been more relevant, especially for those brave enough to embark on a career change. Gone are the days when a single degree or skillset could sustain an entire career. The modern professional landscape demands adaptability and a commitment to lifelong learning.

For career changers, this presents both a challenge and an unprecedented opportunity. The challenge lies in bridging the gap between your current expertise and the requirements of your desired field. The opportunity? A wealth of accessible resources that can transform you from novice to knowledgeable professional in less time than ever before.

Online courses and certifications have emerged as the career changer's secret weapon. These flexible, often self-paced learning options offer a direct route to acquiring industry-specific knowledge and skills. They're not just about adding another line to your resume; they're about building the confidence and competence to thrive in your new chosen field.

In this chapter, we'll explore how to leverage these powerful tools to build your expertise strategically. We'll dive into selecting the right courses, maximizing your learning experience, and translating your newly acquired knowledge into tangible career advancement. Whether you're pivoting to tech, transitioning to healthcare, or venturing into any other field, the path to expertise is at your fingertips.

Remember, in the race of career development, it's not about where you start—it's about your willingness to learn and grow. Let's unlock the potential of continuous learning and set you on the fast track to becoming an expert in your new career.

## Identify Key Skills: Your Career Change Compass

When you're changing careers, figuring out what skills you need is like solving a puzzle. It's exciting, but it can also feel overwhelming. Where do you even start? It's all about becoming a bit of a detective.

First, Job postings are gold mines of information. Spend some time reading through them, and you'll begin to notice patterns emerge. Sarah, a teacher I worked with, decided to switch to data science. She methodically combed through dozens of job listings and tracked the skills they mentioned. By the end, she had a clear picture of what she needed to learn - Python was at the top of her list.

Job postings don't tell the whole story. That's why it's so valuable to talk to people already working in the field. John, who was moving from sales to UX design, went to industry meetups and was probably feeling a bit out of place. However, he struck up a conversation with Elena, a senior designer. She gave him insights you just can't get from a job ad, like the importance of prototyping skills. That conversation completely reshaped John's learning priorities.

Professional associations often have detailed frameworks that break down all the skills you may need. It's like having a cheat sheet for your new career. Healthcare professionals transitioning to health informatics use these resources to great effect.

In addition, you have to keep an eye on trends, too. The job market is always evolving, and sometimes the most in-demand skills aren't even in the job descriptions yet. A few years ago, data visualization wasn't an important skill but now, it's huge. Career changers who spotted this trend early really gave themselves an edge.

While you're focusing on these new skills to learn, don't sell yourself short on what you already know. Your current experience may be valuable, even if it seems unrelated. I love the story of Miguel, a chef who decided to become a software developer. At first, he thought his background was irrelevant, but then he realized his experience in high-pressure, team-based environments was perfect for agile development. It became his unique selling point in interviews.

As you're working through all this, you'll start to see that some skills are absolute requirements, while others are more like nice-to-haves. In cybersecurity, for instance, you might come across many specialized skills, but without a solid grasp of networking basics, you're going to struggle to get your foot in the door.

Remember, identifying these key skills isn't a one-and-done activity. It's more like an ongoing conversation you're having with the industry. Keep your ear to the ground, stay curious, and be ready to adapt. That way, you're not just preparing for your new career - you're setting yourself up to succeed in it.

So, as you start piecing together your skill puzzle, think of it as creating a roadmap to your future. Every skill you identify is a stepping stone on your path. It's not just about ticking boxes; it's about strategically building the expertise that will make you stand out in your new field. If you put in the groundwork now, you'll thank yourself later when you step into your new role.

## Find The Perfect Learning Launchpad

Choosing where to learn online is like picking a gym for your mind - you want one with the right equipment, good trainers, and a vibe that keeps you coming back.

When I first dipped my toes into online learning for my transition into coaching, I felt like a kid in a candy store but also very apprehensive. There were so many options!

One person was dead set on learning data science and jumped at the first course she found. Three weeks and a few hundred dollars later, she realized the content was outdated and the instructor was about as engaging as watching paint dry.

That's why I always tell career changers to do a bit of window shopping before they commit. Platforms like Coursera and edX are like the Ivy Leagues of online learning. They partner with top universities and offer courses that can make your resume light up an inbox.

LinkedIn Learning is another gem. It's like having a direct line to industry experts. Plus, completing courses there is a great way to spruce up your LinkedIn profile.

Udemy and Skillshare are bustling marketplaces where you can find some hidden treasures. I once found a niche course there sustainable architecture that kickstarted a friend's career change.

In addition, Khan Academy is free (I love free). It's perfect for brushing up on fundamentals or exploring new fields without breaking the bank.

The key is to poke around. Read reviews, check out sample lessons, and see if the course content aligns with the skills you identified earlier. It's like trying on shoes - what fits perfectly for someone else might give you blisters.

Jason was transitioning from teaching to web development. He actually signed up for courses on three different platforms before finding his groove. "It was like Goldilocks," he told me, laughing. "This one was too basic, that one was too advanced, but this one's web development track was just right."

So, don't be afraid to shop around. Your perfect learning launchpad is out there, ready to propel you into your new career. Just make sure it's reputable, up-to-date, and speaks your language. When you find the right fit, you'll know it. You'll be itching to log in and learn, and before you know it, you'll be well on your way to mastering those new skills.

## Balancing Your Budget and Your Ambitions: The Free vs. Paid Course Dilemma

Money and learning are topics that can make even the most enthusiastic career changer break out in a cold sweat. But don't worry, we're going to break it down in a way that makes sense for your wallet and your aspirations.

In online learning, you'll find a buffet of options ranging from totally free to "maybe I should sell my car" expensive. The trick is finding that sweet spot where quality meets affordability.

Free courses can be a goldmine. They're perfect for dipping your toes into a new field or brushing up on basics. I've seen people completely change their career trajectory after taking a free intro course. Hector stumbled upon a free graphic design fundamentals course and discovered a passion he never knew he had. Now he's running his own design studio. One course awakened a passion he had and made it easy and exciting to learn more.

However, free courses are often just the tip of the iceberg. They'll give you a taste, but for the main course, you might need to open your wallet.

Paid courses often come with perks that can justify their price tag-- personalized feedback, industry-recognized certificates, and sometimes even job placement assistance. Mia, who transitioned from hospitality to cybersecurity, told me, "The paid course I took was worth every penny. The hands-on labs and mentor support made all the difference in landing my first tech job."

Not everyone has a big budget for learning. If that's you, don't sweat it. There are plenty of ways to get quality education without breaking the bank. Some platforms offer financial aid or scholarships. Others have subscription models that can save you money if you're planning to take multiple courses.

The key is to think of this as an investment in yourself. It's not just about the money you're spending now, but the doors it could open in the future. That said, don't fall into the trap of thinking the most expensive course is automatically the best. I've seen $50 courses that pack more punch than some $500 ones.

Do your homework. Read reviews, evaluate the syllabus, and see if the skills taught align with what you need for your career change. It's okay to start small. Maybe begin with a free course to test the waters, then gradually invest in more comprehensive programs as you get clearer on your path.

At the end of the day, whether you go free or paid, what matters most is your commitment to learning. I've seen people work wonders with free resources and determination. I've also seen people get incredible value from paid programs that fast-tracked their career change.

Your learning journey is uniquely yours. Trust your gut, do your research, and choose the path that feels right for you and your bank account. Remember, every bit of knowledge you gain is a step closer to your new career.

## Charting Your Learning Path: Strategic Course Selection

Selecting the right courses is crucial in your career transition journey. It's about aligning your learning with your professional aspirations and current skill level. Let's explore how to make those choices count.

When Alexis decided to pivot from finance to renewable energy, she approached course selection like a strategic investment. "I looked at my target roles and worked backward," she explained. This method led her to a mix of technical courses on solar technology and broader classes on energy policy.

Consider your starting point. Are you a complete novice or do you have some foundational knowledge? This will guide whether you begin with introductory courses or dive into more advanced material.

Start with fundamental courses that give you a solid grounding in your new field. Then, progressively add more specialized or advanced courses. This approach builds your knowledge systematically and boosts your confidence along the way.

Marco, transitioning from retail to supply chain management, adopted this strategy. He began with a broad introductory course on supply chain principles before tackling more specific topics like inventory optimization and logistics technology.

Don't overlook the power of complementary skills. While focusing on core competencies is essential, courses that develop adjacent skills can set you apart. For instance, a data visualization course might complement your primary focus on business analytics.

Lena, moving from event planning to environmental consulting, took a course on Geographic Information Systems (GIS) on a whim. "It wasn't strictly necessary," she admitted, "but it became my secret weapon in interviews. Companies were impressed by my ability to map environmental data."

As you select courses, keep an eye on industry trends. Emerging technologies or methodologies in your target field should inform your choices. This forward-thinking approach ensures your skills remain relevant.

Regularly review job postings in your desired role. Note any recurring skills or certifications mentioned. Use this information to guide your course selection, ensuring you're learning what employers need.

Remember, course selection isn't a one-time decision. As you progress, you'll gain insights that might shift your focus. Be prepared to adjust your learning plan accordingly.

Carlos, transitioning to UX research, found his interests evolving as he learned. "I started with general UX courses, but as I delved deeper, I discovered a passion for accessibility design. I ended up specializing in that area, which really differentiated my skill set."

Lastly, don't underestimate the value of practical, hands-on courses. Look for options that include projects, case studies, or simulations. These provide tangible experiences you can showcase to potential employers.

Your course selection strategy should be as dynamic and purposeful as your career change itself. By thoughtfully choosing courses that align with your goals, build on each other, and respond to industry needs, you're not just learning – you're crafting a compelling narrative of your professional evolution.

## Course Reviews and Ratings

Course reviews and ratings serve as your compass, helping you navigate toward high-quality educational experiences for your unique needs.

Think of them as insider tips from fellow travelers on your learning journey offering a window into the real-world impact of a course, beyond the polished course descriptions. However, as is the case with any tool, reviews are most useful when you know how to use them skillfully.

### Quantitative Insights: The Power of Numbers

Start with the overall rating. A course consistently rated 4.5 stars or higher across hundreds of reviews often signals quality content and effective instruction. However, don't stop there. Dig deeper into the rating distribution.

Be wary of courses with 5-star and 1-star reviews but few in between. This polarization might indicate a course that works brilliantly for some but falls flat for others. Consider whether you align more closely with the enthusiasts or the critics based on their comments. Consider considering other courses if you aren't sure or contacting the instructor through LinkedIn

### Qualitative Gold: Mining the Comments

While star ratings provide a quick gauge, the real treasure lies in the written reviews. Look for specific, detailed feedback about the course structure, content relevance, and instructor engagement.

Amelia, transitioning from journalism to financial analysis, was torn between two seemingly similar courses. A detailed review of one course mentioned its excellent coverage of financial modeling in Excel – a skill Amelia knew was crucial but hadn't considered. This insight guided her choice and ultimately accelerated her career shift.

## Red Flags and Green Lights

Pay attention to recurring themes in reviews. Are multiple students praising the practical assignments? That's a green light for hands-on learners. Do you see frequent complaints about outdated content? That's a red flag in fast-evolving fields.

In tech-related courses, prioritize recent reviews. A course highly rated two years ago may have lost its edge if not regularly updated. Conversely, a course with improved recent ratings might indicate responsive instructors who continually refine their material.

## Beyond the Platform: Seeking Diverse Perspectives

Don't limit yourself to reviews on the course platform. Explore professional forums, LinkedIn discussions, or Reddit threads where learners share their experiences more candidly.

Diego was pivoting to digital marketing and found a goldmine of information in a marketing professionals' Slack channel. "The unfiltered opinions there gave me a much clearer picture of which certifications carried weight in the industry," he shared.

## The Instructor Factor

Look for reviews that specifically comment on the instructor's teaching style, responsiveness, and expertise. A great course can be elevated by an engaging instructor, while a poor one can diminish even the most promising syllabus.

Remember, the goal isn't to find a perfect course suited to everyone – that's rarely possible. Instead, use reviews and ratings to find the best fit for your learning style, career goals, and existing skill level.

By mastering the art of interpreting course reviews and ratings, you're not just choosing a course; you're strategically investing in your future. This discerning approach ensures that every learning experience brings you one step closer to your new career aspirations.

# Vetting An Online Instructor

An instructor is like a conductor orchestrating your learning experience. Their expertise, or lack thereof, can make the difference between a transformative educational journey and a forgettable one.

When Olivia decided to transition from architecture to sustainable urban planning, she knew the caliber of her instructors would be crucial. She didn't just want knowledge; she craved insights from those shaping the field. Her diligence in researching instructors paid off when she found a course led by a renowned urban planner who had transformed several major cities.

Start by scrutinizing the instructor's professional background. Look for a track record of real-world accomplishments in the field they're teaching. Do they hold or have they held leadership positions in relevant companies or government agencies? Have they contributed to significant projects or innovations?

Zane, a former chef exploring a move into renewable energy, stumbled upon a course taught by a pioneer in solar technology. The instructor had not only founded a successful solar energy company but had also advised governments on renewable energy policies. Zane knew he'd be learning from someone with both theoretical knowledge and practical experience.

Don't just take the course description at face value. Do some detective work. Look up the instructor's publications, patents, or speaking engagements. These can be indicators of their standing in the industry and their commitment to staying current in their field. LinkedIn can be very valuable for this.

Academic credentials are valuable, too, but in many fields, especially rapidly evolving ones, recent industry experience can be equally if not more important. A mix of both is often the sweet spot. Maya, transitioning from retail management to AI ethics, found her ideal instructor in a computer science professor who also consulted for major tech companies on ethical AI implementation.

Consider the instructor's teaching experience as well. While industry heavyweights bring valuable insights, their expertise doesn't always translate to effective teaching. Look for evidence of their ability to communicate complex ideas clearly. Student testimonials can be particularly revealing in this aspect.

Social proof can be a powerful indicator of an instructor's credibility. Check if they have a significant following on professional networks or if they're frequently cited in industry publications. Liam, pivoting to fintech, chose a blockchain course after noticing the instructor was consistently quoted in reputable finance journals.

Remember, the best instructors do more than just impart knowledge – they inspire and, sometimes mentor. They should be able to contextualize the course material within the broader industry landscape and provide insights into emerging trends.

Lastly, don't shy away from reaching out directly to instructors with questions before enrolling. Their responsiveness and the quality of their answers can give you a taste of what to expect from the course. That helped me to decide on a coaching program when I made my transition from recruiting to job search coaching.

By carefully vetting your online instructors, you're not just ensuring a quality education; you're potentially gaining a valuable addition to your professional network. The right instructor can become a mentor, a reference, or even a connection to future opportunities in your new field. Choose wisely, and let these maestros guide you in composing the next movement of your career symphony.

## Course Scheduling and Career Transitions

When you're orchestrating a career change, timing isn't just important— it's everything. The flexibility of online courses can be a game-changer, but it's crucial to understand the rhythm of each learning opportunity.

Nadia, a busy restaurant manager wanting to change to a career in sustainable fashion, initially felt overwhelmed at the prospect of adding study to her packed schedule. However, she discovered a self-paced course in textile sustainability that allowed her to digest lectures during her commute and complete assignments on her day off. "It felt like the course was designed for my life," she beamed.

Not all online courses offer this level of flexibility. Some operate on a fixed schedule, mimicking traditional classroom structures. These can be ideal for learners who thrive on routine and deadlines. Taro was transitioning from graphic design to UX research and found that a structured course with weekly live sessions kept him accountable and connected with peers on a similar journey.

Before you commit, take a hard look at your current obligations. Can you carve out specific time slots for learning, or do you need the freedom to study in sporadic bursts? Be honest with yourself—there's no virtue in signing up for a rigidly scheduled course if you know you'll struggle to attend regular sessions.

Some platforms offer a hybrid approach. Ava, pivoting from event planning to digital marketing, chose a program that combined self-paced modules with optional live Q&A sessions. This format gave her the flexibility she needed while still providing opportunities for real-time interaction with instructors.

Don't underestimate the power of deadlines, even in flexible courses. Marco, moving from sales to data analytics, initially loved the idea of a completely self-paced program. But he soon found himself procrastinating. He course-corrected by setting personal deadlines and treating them as seriously as work commitments.

Consider your learning style, too. Some people absorb information best in concentrated bursts, while others prefer to spread their learning over time. Zara, transitioning to environmental law, discovered she retained complex legal concepts better when she studied in short, daily sessions rather than long weekend crams.

If you're juggling work and study, look for courses that offer mobile-friendly content. Leo, a nurse exploring a move into health informatics, found a course that delivered bite-sized lessons via an app. He could easily fit in 15 minutes of learning during breaks at the hospital.

Remember, flexibility isn't just about when you study—it's also about how you engage with the material. Some courses offer multiple formats for the same content—video lectures, transcripts, and audio versions. This versatility can be a lifesaver when your schedule or energy levels fluctuate. Lastly, don't be afraid to reach out to course providers about flexibility options. Yasmin, transitioning from teaching to corporate training, found that a course she was interested in offered extended deadlines for working professionals—a detail not advertised on their main page.

By carefully considering the tempo of each course and how it aligns with your life's existing rhythms, you're setting yourself up for success. The right balance of structure and flexibility can turn your learning journey from a stressful juggling act into a harmonious part of your daily life. Remember, the goal isn't just to complete courses—it's to absorb and apply new knowledge as you compose the next movement of your career. Choose wisely, and let your learning dance in step with your life.

## Engaging Your Mind with Immersive Learning Experiences

Passive consumption of information is out, and active engagement is in. Interactive elements in online courses aren't just bells and whistles—they're powerful tools that can transform your learning from a spectator sport into an immersive experience. These features can supercharge your career change journey.

When Ravi decided to pivot from accounting to user experience design, he was initially skeptical about online learning. "I thought I'd just be watching videos," he admitted. But the course he chose surprised him with its array of interactive elements. Weekly design challenges pushed him to apply theories to real-world scenarios, while peer review sessions honed his critical eye. "It wasn't just learning; it was doing," Ravi explained. "By the end, I had a portfolio of work I was proud to show potential employers."

Quizzes and assessments, when thoughtfully designed, do more than test your memory—they reinforce learning and highlight areas that need more attention. Sophia, transitioning from marketing to data analytics, found that regular coding quizzes in her Python course helped her identify and fix gaps in her understanding before they became roadblocks.

Discussion forums can be goldmines of insight and networking opportunities. Aisha, moving from teaching to corporate training, initially underestimated the value of her course's discussion board. But she soon found herself engaged in rich debates about learning theories with peers from diverse industries. "Those discussions challenged my thinking and exposed me to perspectives I'd never considered," Aisha reflected. "Plus, I built a network that proved invaluable in my job search."

Look for courses that incorporate real-world projects or simulations. Leon, shifting from retail management to supply chain logistics, chose a course that included a virtual supply chain management game. "It was like a flight simulator for logistics," he laughed. "I made mistakes and learned from them in a risk-free environment. That experience gave me the confidence to apply for roles I might have otherwise thought were out of reach."

Some platforms offer peer-to-peer learning opportunities. Mia, transitioning to environmental science, found tremendous value in her course's peer grading system for lab reports. "Reviewing others' work and receiving constructive feedback on my own deepened my unerstanding in ways that solo study never could," she noted.

Interactive case studies can bring complex concepts to life. Jamal, moving from finance to healthcare administration, praised his course's branching scenario exercises. "We'd work through real healthcare dilemmas, making decisions and seeing their impacts unfold. It made the ethical and practical challenges of the field tangible," he explained.

Don't overlook the power of gamification in learning. Elena, pivoting to cybersecurity, chose a course that turned hacking challenges into a points-based competition. "It tapped into my competitive side," she grinned. "I found myself putting in extra hours, not because I had to, but because I wanted to climb the leaderboard." I found the same thing with the gamified coaching program I attended. I wanted to get the most points all the time.

Remember, the most effective interactive elements are those that mirror real-world tasks in your target field. Yuki, transitioning to data journalism, valued her course's interactive data visualization tools. "Creating infographics and interactive dashboards as assignments meant I was building exactly the skills I'd need on the job," she observed.

By embracing courses rich with interactive elements, you're not just consuming information—you're actively constructing knowledge and skills. This hands-on approach can accelerate your learning, boost your confidence, and provide tangible evidence of your new capabilities. As you evaluate courses, look for those that go beyond passive content delivery to offer a truly engaging learning experience. After all, in the rapidly evolving job market, it's not just what you know—it's how effectively you can apply that knowledge that sets you apart.

## Collecting Digital Badges (Certifications)

In the landscape of career transitions, certificates and credentials are more than just virtual gold stars—they're tangible proof of your evolving expertise. Let's explore how these digital accolades can become powerful tools in your professional reinvention toolkit.

When Priya decided to leap from hospitality management to digital marketing, she knew she needed more than enthusiasm to land a job in her new career. She strategically chose courses that offered recognized certifications. "Each cert became a building block of my credibility," Priya shared. "They weren't just lines on my resume; they were conversation starters in interviews, proving I was serious about my new direction."

The gravitas of a certification often depends on its issuer. Raj, transitioning from sales to data analytics, prioritized courses from tech giants and renowned universities. "Having a data science certificate from Google on my LinkedIn profile opened doors I didn't even know existed," he marveled. "Recruiters started reaching out to me before I even finished my transition."

Not all certifications are created equal. Amina, pivoting from journalism to UX writing, learned this the hard way. "I initially chased quantity over quality," she admitted. "It wasn't until I earned an industry-recognized UX certification that I saw a real shift in how potential employers perceived my skills."

Some credentials go beyond mere completion, offering different levels of mastery. Lucas, moving from teaching to cybersecurity, found that his chosen platform offered tiered certifications. "Starting with the foundational cert gave me confidence, but achieving the expert-level certification is what ultimately landed me my first cybersecurity role," he reflected.

Don't underestimate the power of micro-credentials. Zoe, transitioning to sustainable fashion design, accumulated a series of badges in specific areas like ethical sourcing and eco-friendly textiles. "Together, these micro-credentials told a compelling story of my expertise and passion," Zoe explained. "They showed I wasn't just interested in fashion, but in revolutionizing it."

Some certifications require renewal or continuing education, which can be a blessing in disguise. Alana, shifting from finance to AI ethics, found that maintaining her machine learning certification kept her knowledge cutting-edge. "In a field evolving as rapidly as AI, having a credential that forces me to stay updated is invaluable," she noted.

Remember, certifications can also be stepping stones to more advanced credentials. Jamal started his transition from retail to cloud computing with basic AWS certifications. "Each cert built my confidence and knowledge, preparing me for more advanced qualifications. Now, I'm working towards solutions architect certification, something I couldn't have imagined when I started," he beamed.

While certifications are valuable, how you showcase them also matters. Yoshi, moving into data visualization, created an online portfolio featuring projects from her certified courses. "The certs got me noticed, but it was the actual work I could show that sealed the deal in interviews," he shared.

Don't forget to leverage your new credentials within your current role, if possible. Marcos, transitioning from operations to project management, applied his newly certified skills in his existing job. "Demonstrating my new abilities in a familiar context made my transition feel more natural, both to me and to potential employers," he explained.

In the digital age, your collection of certificates and credentials becomes a passport to new career territories. They verify your skills, demonstrate your commitment, and can often be the tiebreaker in a competitive job market. As you navigate your career change, choose your certifications wisely,
showcase them proudly, and let them open doors to opportunities you might have once thought were out of reach. Remember, in the journey of professional reinvention, these digital badges are not just endpoints—they're launchpads to your next adventure.

## Nurturing Your Career Through Lifelong Learning

Learning isn't a finite task, completed after graduation from a high school, college or university. It is a perpetual journey. The courses you take today are just the first steps on an endless path of growth and discovery.

When Aisha pivoted from elementary education to corporate training, she initially thought a few courses would suffice. "I quickly realized that learning in the corporate world is like trying to hit a moving target," she chuckled. Aisha now dedicates time each week to exploring new training methodologies and emerging workplace trends. "It's not just about staying relevant; it's about staying ahead," she explained.

The tech sector exemplifies the need for continuous learning. Ravi, who transitioned from accounting to software development, found that his learning curve didn't flatten after landing his first coding job—it steepened. "Languages and frameworks I learned during my transition were evolving or being replaced within months," Ravi shared. He now treats learning as part of his job description, regularly participating in coding challenges and contributing to open-source projects to keep his skills sharp.

For some, continuous learning becomes a competitive advantage. Zoe, moved from retail management to sustainable supply chain consulting. She makes it a point to attend industry conferences and workshops regularly.

"Each event gives me new insights to bring back to my clients," Zoe noted. "It's become my secret weapon for delivering innovative solutions."

The rise of micro-learning platforms has made continuous education more accessible than ever. Elena, who switched from marketing to data analytics, swears by bite-sized daily lessons. "Fifteen minutes of learning during my commute adds up to a substantial knowledge boost over time," she explained. "It's like compound interest for your brain."

Networking can be a powerful driver of continuous learning. Jamal, who transitioned from finance to healthcare administration, joined several professional associations in his new field. "The webinars, mentorship programs, and peer discussions have been invaluable," Jamal reflected. "They expose me to real-world challenges and solutions I might not encounter in formal courses."

Some professionals turn their learning journey into a personal brand. Yuki, who moved from journalism to UX research, started a blog documenting her ongoing education in user experience. "Sharing what I learn not only reinforces my understanding but has also positioned me as a thought leader in my new field," Yuki beamed.

Remember, continuous learning isn't always about acquiring new skills—sometimes it's about deepening existing ones. Marcus, who shifted from sales to environmental consulting, focuses on mastering the nuances of his field. "There's always another layer to uncover, another perspective to consider," he mused. "The depth of my knowledge has become my differentiator."

The beauty of continuous learning is its ability to open unexpected doors. Priya, who initially moved from hospitality to digital marketing, found her learning journey leading her into the emerging field of AI-driven customer experience. "If I hadn't stayed curious and kept learning, I might have missed this exciting new direction," she reflected.

Embracing lifelong learning requires a mindset shift. It's about viewing every experience as an opportunity for growth. Liam, who transitioned from teaching to organizational psychology, put it beautifully: "I've stopped seeing myself as having a career. Instead, I'm on a continuous learning expedition, with each role and project as a new exploration."

As you navigate your career change, remember that your initial courses are just the beginning. The most successful career transitioners are those who view learning not as a means to an end, but as an integral part of their professional identity. By cultivating a habit of continuous learning, you're not just keeping pace with your new industry—you're positioning yourself to shape its future. In the ever-evolving world of work, the most valuable skill you can develop is the ability to learn, unlearn, and relearn. So, embrace the journey, stay curious, and let your love for learning propel you to new heights in your reinvented career.

## The Hidden Power of Course Communities

When you sign up for an online course, you're not just getting access to knowledge—you're often opening the door to a vibrant community of like-minded professionals. This network can become the secret ingredient in your career change recipe.

Lena never expected that a simple "Hello" in a course discussion forum would change the trajectory of her career transition. Shifting from event planning to UX design, she found herself in a lively debate about user personas with a fellow student. "That conversation led to a virtual coffee chat, which turned into a mentorship, and eventually a job referral," Lena shared, still amazed at how a single interaction snowballed into a career-defining opportunity.

For Raj, the course community became his sounding board. "Whenever I hit a coding roadblock, there was always someone online who'd faced a similar challenge," he explained. "The collective brainpower of the group was like having a 24/7 support team." Raj's proactive engagement in helping others solve problems not only cemented his own learning but also built his reputation within the community.

The diversity in online course communities can be eye-opening. Zhao began transitioning to blockchain technology. He found himself collaborating on projects with students from across the globe. "Working with a developer from Estonia and a financial analyst from Brazil on a decentralized app project gave me insights I never would have gained in a traditional classroom," he marveled. These cross-cultural connections expanded not just his technical skills, but her global perspective.

Some savvy career changers use course communities as a launchpad for their personal branding efforts. Marcus started a study group within his course. "Organizing weekly discussions positioned me as a leader in our little community," he reflected. "It boosted my confidence and gave me a taste of thought leadership in my new field."

Don't underestimate the power of shared struggles. When Aisha felt overwhelmed transitioning to cybersecurity, the empathy and encouragement from her course peers kept her going. "Knowing others were navigating similar challenges made the journey less lonely," she said. "We celebrated each other's wins and supported each other through the tough times."

For some, course communities become incubators for innovation. Zoe and a group of fellow students turned their final project into a real-world startup. "We all brought different skills to the table—design, supply chain, marketing. The course gave us a safe space to experiment, and before we knew it, we had a viable business model," Zoe explained, now the proud co-founder of an eco-friendly clothing line.

Remember, networking in course communities isn't just about making friends—it's about strategic relationship building. Elena made it a point to connect with students who complemented her skills. "I sought out those with technical backgrounds to balance my policy expertise," she shared. "These relationships have led to collaborative research projects that are shaping my new career path."

Don't limit your networking just to peers. Many courses feature guest lectures or Q&A sessions with industry experts. Hannah made a lasting impression during one such session. "I asked a thoughtful question that sparked a lengthy discussion. The speaker ended up inviting me to contribute to his healthcare policy blog," she recounted, still amazed at how a single interaction opened up a world of opportunities.

As you embark on your learning journey, remember that the true value of a course often lies as much in its community as in its content. Engage actively, share generously, and be open to unexpected connections. In the tapestry of your career transition, these digital threads of community can weave a strong support network, spark innovative ideas, and even become the bridge to your next professional opportunity. After all, in the interconnected world of modern careers, it's not just what you know, but who you know—and who knows you—that can make all the difference.

## Crafting A Career Mosaic Through Blended Learning

In the quest for career reinvention, relying on a single source of knowledge is like trying to paint a masterpiece with just one color. The true artists of career transition know the power of blending various learning experiences to create a rich, nuanced skillset.

Helen's journey from corporate law to environmental policy wasn't a straight line—it was a tapestry woven from diverse learning experiences. "I started with a foundational online course in environmental science, but I quickly realized I needed more," she recalled. Olivia supplemented her learning with a series of workshops on climate legislation, a hands-on field course in ecological assessment, and even a stint volunteering with a local conservation group. "Each experience added a new dimension to my understanding. The combination made me a much more versatile and attractive candidate in my new field," she explained.

For Santi transitioning to renewable energy engineering, the key was finding complementary resources. He paired a comprehensive online certification in solar technology with a series of short courses on energy storage systems. "The certification gave me the core knowledge, but the supplementary courses helped me understand the cutting-edge developments in the field," Santi noted. He also attended industry webinars and virtual conferences, which exposed him to real-world applications and networking opportunities.

The beauty of combining sources is the ability to fill specific skill gaps. When Naomi decided to pivot from event planning to supply chain logistics, she identified analytics as a crucial skill she lacked. "I took a specialized course in supply chain analytics to complement my broader logistics certification," Naomi shared. "This targeted approach allowed me to compete with candidates who had years of industry experience."

Some career changers find value in unconventional learning combinations. Akira, moving from culinary arts to food science, mixed formal online courses with hands-on experiments in his own kitchen. "I'd learn about molecular gastronomy in my course, then immediately try out the concepts at home," he chuckled. "This blend of theory and practice not only cemented my learning but also gave me unique insights that impressed potential employers."

For those on a budget, a strategic combination of free and paid resources can yield impressive results. Fatima, transitioning to blockchain development, started with free coding bootcamps and open-source learning materials. She then invested in a specialized blockchain certification to round out her skills. "The free resources gave me a solid foundation, while the paid certification provided the specific expertise and credibility I needed to break into the field," Fatima explained.

Don't underestimate the power of cross-disciplinary learning. When Theo decided to move to sustainable investing, he didn't just focus on investment strategies. He also delved into environmental science and corporate sustainability through a variety of MOOCs and webinars. "This interdisciplinary approach gave me a unique perspective that set me apart in interviews," he reflected. "I could speak the language of both finance and sustainability fluently."

Remember, combining sources isn't just about accumulating knowledge—it's about creating a unique value proposition. Yasmin, augmented reality (AR) development, curated a learning path that included technical courses, design thinking workshops, and even a class on storytelling. "This eclectic mix allowed me to approach AR development from multiple angles," Yasmin said. "I'm not just a coder or a designer—I'm a holistic AR experience creator."

As you navigate your career transition, think of your learning journey as a customizable adventure. Mix and match courses, certifications, workshops, and hands-on experiences to create a knowledge base that's uniquely yours. This multifaceted approach not only makes you a more well-rounded professional but also demonstrates your initiative and adaptability—qualities highly prized in today's dynamic job market.

In the end, your diverse learning experiences will come together like pieces of a puzzle, revealing a picture of expertise that's far greater than the sum of its parts. So, be bold in your choices, eclectic in your learning, and watch as your career transition transforms from a simple change to a remarkable evolution.

Practice and Apply What You Learn

Knowledge without experience practicing and applying what you learn is like a car without fuel—it looks great, but it won't take you anywhere. Isabelle's transition to bioinformatics wasn't just about absorbing information—it was about bringing it to life. "I could have just completed the courses and called it a day, but I knew that wouldn't be enough," she recalled. Isabelle took her learning a step further by volunteering to help a local research lab analyze genetic data. "That real-world experience was invaluable. It not only solidified my understanding but gave me concrete examples to discuss in interviews," she explained, beaming with pride.

For Omar, moving to renewable energy sales, the key was creating opportunities for himself. He didn't wait for the perfect internship to fall into his lap. Instead, he approached a small solar panel installation company in his neighborhood. "I offered to create a marketing strategy for them, pro bono. They were hesitant at first, but my enthusiasm won them over," Omar chuckled. That volunteer project not only honed his skills but also led to his first paid position.

Sometimes, the most valuable practical experience comes from personal projects. When Lila decided to game development, she didn't just rely on coding bootcamps. She challenged herself to create a simple mobile game from scratch. "It was frustrating at times, but incredibly rewarding," Lila shared. "That game became my portfolio piece, demonstrating not just my technical skills but also my creativity and perseverance."

Niko took a unique approach to gaining hands-on experience in his transition from retail to cybersecurity. He set up a home lab to practice ethical hacking techniques. "I created various scenarios to test my skills, documenting each step of the process," Niko explained. "This not only reinforced my learning but gave me tangible examples of problem-solving to share with potential employers."

For some, applying their skills can lead to unexpected opportunities. Amara, shifting to brand management, started a blog documenting her learning journey and sharing insights on eco-friendly marketing practices. "What began as a way to reinforce my learning turned into a platform that attracted industry attention," Amara marveled. "I ended up consulting for small businesses before I even landed my first official job in the field."

Don't underestimate the power of collaboration in applied learning. Tareq, transitioning to urban planning, joined an online community of aspiring urban designers. Together, they tackled hypothetical city development challenges. "Working on these projects with peers from around the world not only sharpened my skills but also expanded my perspective on global urban issues," Tareq reflected.

Remember, applied learning isn't just about technical skills—it's also about developing the soft skills crucial in your new field. When Yuki decided to move to environmental consulting, she volunteered for a local conservation group. "Beyond applying my analytical skills to their funding strategies, I learned how to communicate complex ideas to diverse stakeholders—a skill that proved invaluable in my new career," Yuki noted.

For those worried about lacking experience, pro bono work can be a game-changer. Zara, pivoting from teaching to corporate training, offered to redesign the onboarding process for a small non-profit. "It was a win-win situation. They got a fresh perspective on their training needs, and I got hands-on experience designing and implementing a corporate training program," Zara explained. This project became a cornerstone of her portfolio, demonstrating her ability to apply her skills in a business context. As you navigate your career transition, remember that every bit of applied learning adds another brushstroke to the masterpiece of your new professional identity. Whether it's through volunteer work, personal projects, or collaborative challenges, find ways to bring your learning to life. These practical experiences not only reinforce your skills but also build your confidence, expand your network, and provide compelling stories to share with potential employers.

In the end, it's not just about what you know—it's about what you can do with that knowledge. By actively applying your skills, you're not just preparing for your new career; you're already beginning to live it. So, seek out opportunities to put your learning into practice, and watch as your career transition transforms into a reality.

## Fueling Your Career Change by Staying Motivated

Staying motivated through the ups and downs is what separates those who dream from those who achieve. Let's explore how to keep your motivational fires burning bright throughout your journey.

Lucia's transition to environmental law was a marathon, not a sprint. "There were days when I felt like I was climbing an endless mountain," she confessed. Lucia found her motivation by creating a vision board filled with images of courtrooms, pristine forests, and quotes from environmental leaders. "Every morning, I'd look at that board and remind myself why I started this journey. It was my North Star on tough days."

For Alejandro, moving to renewable energy design, motivation came through gamification. He treated his learning journey like a video game, complete with levels, achievements, and rewards. "I'd set weekly goals—finishing a course module, completing a project—and reward myself when I hit them," Alejandro shared with a grin. "My favorite reward was a fancy coffee and an hour of guilt-free gaming. It made the whole process feel like fun rather than work."

Sometimes, motivation comes from a community. When Nadia decided to pivot to fashion design, she joined an online group of fellow career changers. "We had weekly check-ins where we'd share our progress, challenges, and wins," Nadia explained. "Knowing I had to report back to the group kept me accountable, and their support lifted me on days when my motivation flagged."

Kaito found an unconventional way to stay motivated during his transition from sales to biotechnology. He started a YouTube channel documenting his career change journey. "Sharing my experiences publicly gave me a sense of responsibility to my viewers," Kaito reflected. "Their encouragement and curiosity about my progress became a powerful motivator."

For some, motivation is all about the numbers. Yasmin, shifting from graphic design to AI ethics, created a detailed spreadsheet tracking her progress. "I logged hours studied, courses completed, and skills acquired," she explained. "Watching those numbers grow gave me a tangible sense of progress, even on days when I felt stuck."

Remember, setbacks are part of the journey. When Rafiq hit a roadblock in his transition to green building architecture, he found motivation in the stories of others who had successfully changed careers. "I'd listen to podcasts about career pivots during my commute," Rafiq shared. "Hearing how others overcame challenges reminded me that my struggles were normal and surmountable."

Sometimes, motivation comes from giving back to others. Ines, moving to conservation technology, volunteered to teach basic coding to kids at a local nature center. "Seeing their excitement about technology and nature reignited my passion," Ines beamed. "It reminded me of the impact I could have in my new field."

Don't underestimate the power of small wins. When Mateo felt overwhelmed by the scope of his transition from retail management to sustainable supply chain consulting, he broke his goals into tiny, achievable tasks. "I'd celebrate completing a single lesson or writing a paragraph of my capstone project," Mateo explained. "These micro-victories kept my momentum going."

For Aidan, staying motivated during his shift to art therapy meant connecting her learning to real-world impact. She volunteered at a local community center, applying her budding art therapy skills. "Seeing firsthand how these techniques could help people gave my studies a sense of urgency and purpose," Aidan reflected.

As you navigate your career transition, remember that motivation isn't a constant state—it's a practice. Some days it will flow easily, others you'll need to coax it out. The key is to find what resonates with you. Whether it's visual reminders, community support, gamification, or connecting to your bigger "why," build a motivational toolkit that keeps you moving forward.

Your career change is more than just acquiring new skills—it's about becoming a new version of yourself. Each study session, each small victory, is a step towards that new identity. So when motivation wanes, remind yourself of the future you're building. Visualize yourself thriving in your new role, making the impact you've dreamed of.

Remember, the path of career transition is rarely a straight line. There will be twists, turns, and perhaps a few detours. But with a well of motivation to draw from, you'll have the resilience to navigate any challenge. Stay focused, stay inspired, and keep moving forward. Your future self—the one already thriving in your new career—is cheering you on every step of the way.

The landscape of professional development is vast and ever-changing, much like the ocean. Online courses and certifications? They're your trusty vessels, equipped to navigate these waters of change.

Imagine Sophia, a former chef who dreamed of making waves in marine conservation. "At first, the gulf between my culinary skills and marine biology seemed impossibly wide," she confessed. But armed with a curated selection of online courses, Sophia began to bridge that gap. "Each course was like adding a new tool to my belt. Before I knew it, I was speaking the language of conservation with confidence."

These digital credentials aren't just pieces of paper (or pixels, as it were). They're beacons that signal your commitment and capability to potential employers.

The real magic is becoming awakened to the fact that learning doesn't stop when you land a job in your new career. That's when it should kick into high gear. Amy, who pivoted to social media management, put it beautifully: "My certifications got me in the door, but my commitment to continuous learning is what's propelling my career forward."

Think of your career as a grand expedition. Each course, each certification, and each new skill you acquire is another step on this journey. They're not just checkboxes to tick off; they're building blocks of your professional identity.

Remember, adaptability is your superpower. Your willingness to learn, unlearn, and relearn sets you apart in a crowded job market. It's not just about keeping up; it's about staying ahead of the curve.

As you continue on your path of career transition, every online course, every certification, and every new skill you acquire is a testament to your resilience and adaptability. They're proof that you're not bound by your past but are actively shaping your future.

So, as you click the 'Enroll' button for a new course or proudly add a new certification to your LinkedIn profile, know that you're doing more than just accumulating credentials. You're crafting a narrative of growth, adaptability, and determination. You're telling the world – and yourself – that you're ready for whatever challenges your new career may bring.

In the grand tapestry of your professional life, continuous learning must be the thread that ties it all together. Embrace it, relish the challenges, and remember – in the ever-evolving world of careers, the most exciting chapter is always the one you're about to write.

# Step 8:

# Test Drive Your Future: Volunteer and Intern Experiences

Imagine test-driving a car before making a purchase. Now, apply that concept to your career. Volunteering or interning in your field of interest is like taking your future for a spin before fully committing. It's a great strategy that allows you to bridge the gap between your current skill set and the demands of the profession you are switching to.

This hands-on approach serves multiple purposes. First, it provides a realistic preview of the day-to-day realities of your chosen field. You'll get to see the inner workings, experience the challenges, and taste the rewards firsthand. This immersion can either confirm your passion or prompt a timely course correction.

Second, volunteering and interning are opportunities to build a professional network. You'll connect with industry insiders, potential mentors, and fellow aspirants. These relationships can open doors, provide guidance, and offer invaluable insights that textbooks and online research can't match.

Moreover, these experiences allow you to develop and hone specific skills relevant to your target career. You'll have the chance to apply theoretical knowledge in practical situations, learn to navigate real-world complexities, and problem-solve on the fly.

Lastly, volunteer work and internships bolster your resume, demonstrating initiative, commitment, and relevant experience to potential employers. In a competitive job market, this practical experience can be the differentiator that sets you apart from other candidates.

In the following sections, we'll explore how to find the right opportunities, make the most of your experience, and leverage these experiences in your career journey. Remember, every successful professional started somewhere – and many began by volunteering or interning in their field of interest.

## Spotting Golden Opportunities

The quest for the right volunteer or internship position is like a treasure hunt. Your map? The vast landscape of organizations, associations, nonprofits, and companies related to your aspired career. Your treasure? The invaluable experience and connections waiting to be discovered.

Start by casting a wide net. Let's say you're interested in environmental science. Your research might lead you to local wildlife preservation societies, national parks, environmental policy think tanks, or even green technology startups. Each of these could offer a unique perspective on the field.

Sarah, a mid-career professional looking to transition into nonprofit management, began by volunteering at her local food bank on weekends. This experience not only gave her insight into nonprofit operations but also connected her with a board member who later became her mentor.

Don't limit yourself to traditional internships. Many organizations offer "micro-internships" or project-based opportunities. For instance, a marketing student might find a short-term gig helping a small business revamp its social media strategy.

Remember, not all valuable experiences come with a paycheck. Unpaid positions can be goldmines of experience, especially in competitive fields. Tom volunteered to write for his community newsletter. This unpaid gig led to a portfolio of published work, which helped him land a paid internship at a regional newspaper.

If you're currently unemployed, consider throwing yourself fully into a full-time volunteer or internship role. This immersive experience can accelerate your learning and network building. Amanda accepted a three-month unpaid internship at a software startup. The skills she gained made her a competitive candidate for entry-level developer positions.

For those juggling current jobs, part-time opportunities are your best friend. Look for evening or weekend positions, or explore remote volunteering options. Many organizations now offer flexible arrangements to accommodate working professionals.

Pro tip: Don't overlook professional associations in your field. They often have volunteer committees or mentorship programs that can provide both experience and networking opportunities.

Remember, the goal is to find opportunities that align with your career objectives while fitting your current life circumstances. Be creative, be persistent, and be open to unexpected paths – they might just lead to your dream career.

## The Art of Strategic Networking

In the quest for volunteer and internship opportunities, your network is an invaluable resource, often hiding gems of possibilities beneath the surface. It's not just about who you know, but who they know.

Begin by mapping out your existing connections. This includes obvious contacts like former classmates and coworkers, but don't overlook less apparent links. Your neighbor who works in a tangentially related field, or the acquaintance you met at a community event last month, could be unexpected sources of leads.

Alex mentioned his career transition to his dentist during a routine check-up. To his surprise, the dentist's spouse worked for a healthcare analytics firm and helped Alex secure an informational interview, which later led to a part-time internship.

Professional networking platforms can be powerful tools, but use them strategically. Instead of sending generic connection requests, engage meaningfully with content in your desired field. Comment on posts, share insights and join relevant groups. This approach helped Priya catch the attention of a nonprofit director who was impressed by her consistent, thoughtful contributions to discussions about cause marketing.

Don't underestimate the power of informational interviews. Reach out to professionals in your target field, expressing genuine interest in their work and career path. While these conversations may not immediately lead to opportunities, they often plant seeds that bloom later.

Remember, networking is a two-way street. Always consider how you can provide value to your connections, even if it's just sharing an interesting article or making an introduction. This reciprocity builds stronger, more lasting relationships.

Be prepared for a gradual process. Networking rarely yields instant results, and that's okay. Each conversation and connection is a step forward, even if it doesn't immediately translate to a tangible opportunity.

Lastly, keep your network informed about your goals and progress. A simple update email or coffee catch-up can remind your contacts to keep an eye out for relevant opportunities.

Networking for volunteer and internship opportunities is about playing the long game. It's about building genuine relationships, staying curious, and remaining open to unexpected paths. With patience and persistence, your network can become a powerful catalyst for your career transition.

## Tapping into Professional Organizations

In your efforts to develop experience, professional organizations can be treasure troves of opportunities. These industry-specific groups often serve as nexus points for practitioners, enthusiasts, and aspiring professionals.

Many such organizations maintain job boards or opportunity listings that are exclusive to their members. For instance, a budding financial analyst might find the Chartered Financial Analyst (CFA) Institute's career center to be a goldmine of internship postings that aren't advertised elsewhere.

Beyond job listings, these organizations frequently host events, workshops, and conferences. For example, an aspiring graphic designer attended a local chapter meeting of the American Institute of Graphic Arts (AIGA). There, she connected with an art director who offered her a chance to shadow at his agency, leading to a part-time role.

Some professional organizations run mentorship programs, pairing newcomers with experienced professionals. This was the case for Rahul, who joined the Association for Computing Machinery (ACM) as a student member. Through their mentorship program, he was matched with a senior software engineer who not only provided career guidance but also recommended him for an internship at his company.

Don't overlook the potential of smaller, niche organizations. Often, people find a wealth of volunteer opportunities through smaller groups that aren't visible on larger job sites.

Many of these organizations offer student or early-career memberships at reduced rates. While there may be a cost, the networking opportunities and resources often provide a significant return on investment.

Remember to engage actively within these organizations. Volunteer for committees, contribute to newsletters or help organize events. This involvement can set you apart and create organic opportunities for internships or volunteer work.

Lastly, keep an eye on the organization's social media channels and email newsletters. They often announce short-term project opportunities or calls for volunteers that can be perfect for gaining experience.

By strategically engaging with professional organizations in your target field, you're not just finding opportunities - you're immersing yourself in the professional culture and community of your new industry. This holistic approach can provide context and connections that prove invaluable as you navigate your career transition.

# The Art of Tailored Outreach

When trying to find volunteer or internship opportunities, a one-size-fits-all approach rarely works. Instead, think of each application or inquiry as a custom-fitted suit, meticulously crafted to fit the specific organization and role.

Begin by researching the organization you're approaching. Understand their mission, recent projects, and challenges they might be facing. This knowledge allows you to speak their language and demonstrate genuine interest.

For example, Maya was transitioning to user experience design. When applying for a UX internship at an EdTech startup, she drew parallels between designing lesson plans and creating user journeys. By framing her experience this way, she showed how her background could bring value to the role in a way that a screener, an interviewer or a hiring manager would understand.

Your career transition story can be a powerful tool when tailored correctly. Kai used his cover letter to a wildlife preservation group to explain how his data analysis skills could help track endangered species populations. This unexpected angle caught the attention of the volunteer coordinator, leading to a meaningful conversation and eventually, a position.

When highlighting transferable skills, be specific and provide concrete examples. Instead of merely stating "I have strong communication skills," illustrate it with a scenario. For instance, "In my previous role as a customer service representative, I regularly translated complex product information into easily understandable terms for clients, a skill I believe would be valuable in explaining scientific concepts to the public in this outreach role."

Remember to address the organization's needs as well as your own and don't shy away from acknowledging areas where you lack experience. Instead, demonstrate your eagerness to learn and grow. Zara openly discussed her limited knowledge of textile production in her application but emphasized her quick learning ability and passion for the work.

Lastly, follow up on your applications or attempted contacts professionally and persistently. A well-timed, thoughtful follow-up email can sometimes make the difference between being overlooked and landing an opportunity. By carefully tailoring each interaction, you're not just seeking an opportunity - you're building a compelling case for why you're the right person for the role, despite (or even because of) your unique career trajectory.

## Leveraging Your Transferable Skills

Transferable skills are your secret weapons. They're the bridges that span the gap between your past experience and your future aspirations, often proving more valuable than industry-specific knowledge.

Start by conducting a thorough inventory of your skills. Look beyond the obvious and dig deep into your professional and personal experiences. For example, Nadia realized that her years of managing guest complaints had honed her conflict resolution skills - a crucial asset in HR.

When presenting these skills, context is key. Don't just list them; illustrate how they've been applied. For instance, one person highlighted how his ability to distill complex information into compelling narratives would be invaluable with crafting press releases and public statements.

Consider the less obvious connections. Another drew parallels between coordinating a busy kitchen during service and managing multiple project timelines. This unique perspective caught the attention of hiring managers and led to several internship offers.

Adaptability is a powerful transferable skill for career changers. Demonstrate instances where you've successfully navigated change or learned new systems quickly. Fatima was trying to transition to tech sales. She emphasized how she had consistently been the top performer in implementing new point-of-sale systems, showcasing her tech-savviness and adaptability.

Leadership skills are universally valuable. Even if you're not moving into a management role, the ability to take initiative and guide projects is appealing to most organizations. Raj, shifting to corporate training, highlighted how he had led curriculum development teams, demonstrating his capacity for collaborative leadership.

Problem-solving is another universally appreciated skill. Provide specific examples of how you've tackled challenges in your previous roles. Remember, the key is to make explicit connections between your past experiences and the requirements of your target role or industry. Don't assume that the relevance of your skills will be obvious to others - spell it out clearly and confidently in your resume, LinkedIn profile, and on interviews.

By effectively showcasing your transferable skills, you're not just filling gaps in your resume; you're presenting yourself as a well-rounded candidate with a unique perspective and a diverse skill set. This approach can turn what might be seen as a lack of direct experience into a compelling advantage.

## Embrace the Unconventional: The Power of Flexibility

In the pursuit of career transition, being rigid in your thinking can be your greatest obstacle. Embracing flexibility opens doors to more opportunities that can propel you toward your goals.

Consider part-time roles as stepping stones. These positions allow you to dip your toes into your new field while maintaining financial stability through your current job. For instance, a few hours a week at a local nonprofit can provide insights into the social services sector for someone transitioning from another field.

Project-based work offers concentrated bursts of experience. These short-term engagements can rapidly expand your skill set and portfolio. A weekend hackathon can give aspiring developers hands-on coding experience, while a month-long marketing campaign can showcase a budding marketer's creativity.

Virtual volunteering has expanded the range of flexible opportunities. Many organizations now offer positions that can be done from anywhere, at any time. This flexibility is particularly beneficial for those balancing family commitments or full-time employment.

Consider seasonal opportunities. Some industries have peak periods where they need extra hands. These cyclical openings can provide intense, immersive experiences.

Job shadowing and informational interviews can offer insights and networking opportunities. Don't discount these shorter interactions; they can often lead to more substantial opportunities.

Freelance or consulting work allows you to take on varied projects across different organizations. This diversity can help you identify which aspects of your new field resonate most with you.

Remember, each opportunity regardless of scope or duration, is a chance to learn, network, and inch closer to your career goals. By remaining flexible and open-minded, you create a path of diverse experiences that collectively build towards your desired career transition.

Research the Organization

Before submitting any application, immerse yourself in the world of your target organization. This due diligence, not only will help to inform your decision but also equip you with insights for tailoring your approach.

Start with the organization's official channels. Review their website, paying attention to their mission statement, values, business successes, and recent projects. Follow their social media accounts to gauge their public persona and focus areas. If you have an investment account with a firm that offers company and investment research, review the annual and quarterly reports of publicly held companies that are available to you. These can provide concrete data on the organization's stability and growth trajectory.

Dive deeper by exploring industry publications and news articles. These can provide unbiased perspectives on the organization's standing in the field and any recent developments or challenges they may be facing.

Leverage professional networking platforms to identify current or former employees. Reach out respectfully for informational interviews. These conversations can offer insider perspectives on the organization's culture, work environment, and potential growth opportunities.

Attend industry events or webinars where the organization is represented. This can provide a chance to observe their public-facing staff and potentially make direct connections.

If possible, experience the organization as a customer or end-user. This can give you firsthand insight into their products or services and how they operate.

Pay attention to the organization's partners and collaborators. These relationships can indicate the company's values and direction.

Explore employee review sites, but approach these with a balanced perspective. Look for patterns in feedback rather than focusing on individual comments. For example, avoid paying too much attention to horrible reviews from disgruntled employees and those heaping excessive praise on a firm unless you see many of one type or another.

By thoroughly researching the organization, you position yourself to make informed decisions about your career path. This knowledge will demonstrate your genuine interest and commitment during the application process, setting you apart as a well-prepared and enthusiastic candidate.

## Ace the Volunteer and Internship Interview

As you would for any interview, thoroughly review the organization's mission, recent projects, and any challenges they might be facing. For instance, if you're interviewing for a position at a local animal shelter, familiarize yourself with their adoption rates, community outreach programs, and any recent initiatives.

Prepare concise, compelling answers to common questions about your motivation. A former retail manager transitioning to environmental conservation might explain how customer interactions about sustainable products sparked their passion for environmental issues.

Be ready to discuss your transferable skills in the context of the new field. An aspiring museum curator with a background in event planning could highlight how their experience in logistics and timeline management would be valuable in organizing exhibitions.

Research common industry terms and current trends. If you're moving into digital marketing, be prepared to discuss concepts like SEO, content marketing, or the latest social media platform changes.

Prepare thoughtful questions about the role and organization. An intern applicant for a tech startup might ask about the company's approach to product development or plans for scaling.

Practice explaining your career transition journey succinctly and be prepared to discuss your learning goals. For some careers, consider preparing a small portfolio or examples of relevant work, even if it's from personal projects.

Familiarize yourself with the organization's dress code and culture to ensure you present yourself appropriately during the interview.

By thoroughly preparing for these interviews, you will demonstrate your commitment to the opportunity and your potential as an addition to the team, regardless of your background. This preparation sets the stage for a productive conversation about how you and the organization can mutually benefit from the experience.

## Sharpen Your Edge: Strategic Skill Acquisition

During your volunteer or internship experience, approach each day as an opportunity for growth and learning. Actively seek ways to apply and expand your skill set.

Observe the professionals around you, noting the techniques and tools they use. Ask for guidance or resources to improve if you notice a skill gap.

Take initiative in proposing projects that align with your learning goals. For instance, if you're aiming to improve your data analysis skills, you might offer to help compile and interpret the organization's performance metrics.

Don't shy away from challenging assignments or work. Embrace those that push you out of your comfort zone, because these often provide the most significant learning opportunities.

Ask for feedback regularly. Ask your supervisor or colleagues for constructive criticism of your work. Use this input to refine your skills and approach.

Look for cross-departmental collaborations. These experiences can broaden your understanding of how different areas of the organization interact and function.

Keep a learning journal to document new skills, challenges overcome, and insights gained. This record can be valuable for future job applications and interviews.

Take advantage of any formal training or professional development opportunities offered by the organization. These might include workshops, webinars, or industry conferences.

By approaching your experience with a proactive mindset focused on skill acquisition, you maximize the value of your time and position yourself for success in your new career path.

## Cultivate Connections: The Art of On-the-Job Networking

Your internship or volunteer position is not just a learning opportunity, but a prime networking environment. Every interaction is a chance to build relationships that could shape your future career path.

Engage in casual conversations with colleagues during breaks or team events. These informal chats can lead to valuable insights about the industry and potential job openings. For example, a conversation about a colleague's previous work experience might reveal an upcoming project that aligns with your skills. It won't help every time but can over time.

Take an interest in your supervisors' career evolution. Understanding their paths can guide your career progression and might lead to mentorship opportunities.

Participate actively in team meetings, offering thoughtful input when appropriate. This demonstrates your engagement and can catch the attention of decision-makers in the organization.

Attend any company-wide events or industry gatherings that are open to you. Don't do it at every meeting. You can easily become a target of criticism if you offer opinions too often. After all, you're still learning. However, these settings often allow for interactions with professionals from different departments or even other organizations in your field and professional visibility.

If your organization hosts client meetings or vendor presentations, request to sit in when appropriate. These experiences can broaden your understanding of the industry and expand your network beyond your immediate team.

Offer to assist with projects outside your immediate responsibilities. This can introduce you to staff from other departments and showcase your versatility.

Connect with fellow interns or volunteers. Today's peer might be tomorrow's colleague or even employer.

Maintain professionalism in all your interactions, remembering that every conversation could be a stepping stone to future opportunities.

By approaching networking as an integral part of your internship or volunteer experience, you're not just building skills, but also laying the groundwork for a robust professional network in your new field.

## Learning from Feedback

Seeking and implementing feedback is a crucial component of your growth during an internship or volunteer experience. It's not just about improvement; it's about demonstrating your commitment to excellence and your adaptability.

Consider the story of Mahesh, transitioning into urban planning. During his internship at a city development office, he proactively scheduled monthly review sessions with his mentor. In one such meeting, his mentor noted that while Raj's spatial awareness and project coordination skills were excellent, his technical drawing abilities needed refinement. Raj embraced this feedback, enrolled in an online CAD course, and by the end of his internship, was producing detailed urban layouts that his mentor deemed "professional-grade."

Don't limit yourself to formal feedback sessions. Casual conversations can yield valuable insights. Volunteering at a local radio station to gain experience in broadcast journalism, created a habit of asking for quick critiques after each segment produced. This approach led to a pivotal moment when an offhand comment from the station manager helped Zoe realize she had a talent for investigative reporting – a direction she hadn't previously considered.

Be specific when asking for feedback. Instead of a general "How am I doing?", try targeted questions like "How could I improve my data visualization skills?" or "What do you think I should focus on to become more effective in policy analysis?" This approach yielded significant results for Amir, an intern transitioning to renewable energy research. By specifically asking about his scientific writing, he received tailored advice that dramatically improved his ability to draft compelling research proposals.

Remember, feedback isn't always about addressing weaknesses; it can also help you identify and leverage your strengths. Naomi, volunteering at an art gallery to gain curatorial experience, consistently received positive feedback on her ability to engage visitors with compelling artwork descriptions. This insight helped her specialize in educational outreach within the art world, eventually leading to a full-time position at a major museum.

Importantly, don't become an "askhole" and just collect feedback – act on it. Demonstrate your responsiveness by implementing suggestions and circling back to show your progress. This approach impressed Naomi's supervisor, who later remarked that her ability to rapidly incorporate feedback set her apart from other volunteers.

Lastly, consider seeking feedback from peers and colleagues, not just supervisors. Their perspectives can provide valuable insights into your teamwork and collaboration skills.

By actively asking for and thoughtfully implementing feedback, you're not just improving your performance – you're showcasing your dedication to growth and your potential as a valuable long-term asset to the organization and your newly chosen field.

## Crafting a Compelling Portfolio

Documenting your experiences and achievements during your internship or volunteer work is important for demonstrating your growth and newly acquired skills. A well-crafted portfolio can be a powerful tool in your career transition journey.

Lena, transitioning into graphic design, made it a habit to save samples of her work each week, from initial sketches to final designs. She also kept a digital journal, jotting down new techniques she learned and challenges she overcame. By the end of her internship, Lena had compiled a diverse portfolio that showcased her progression from novice to competent designer.

Hassan, volunteering to gain experience with sustainable agriculture, took a different approach. He created a blog documenting a community garden's seasonal changes, pest management techniques, and crop yields. This not only served as a record of his learning but also demonstrated his ability to communicate complex agricultural concepts to a general audience.

Consider creating both physical and digital versions of your portfolio. One person maintained a physical sketchbook of her wireframes and user flow diagrams, which she later digitized and organized into an online portfolio. This dual approach allowed her to showcase both her creative process and her final products.

Don't limit your portfolio to just completed projects. Include documentation of your problem-solving process, collaborative efforts, and even setbacks you've overcome. Javy, transitioning to event planning, included a case study in his portfolio detailing how he salvaged a nearly derailed fundraising event, demonstrating his crisis management skills.

Remember to update your portfolio regularly. Set aside time each week to reflect on your recent experiences and add relevant items. This habit helped Aisha, a budding environmental scientist, track her growing expertise in water quality testing throughout her internship at a local conservation group.

By diligently building and refining your portfolio, you're not just creating a record of your work - you're crafting a compelling narrative of your professional growth and readiness for your new career path.

## Using Others Seal of Approval: The Power of Recommendations

As your internship or volunteer experience draws to a close, securing strong recommendations can be a piece that completes your career transition puzzle. These recommendations serve as powerful testimonials to your newly acquired skills and your potential in your new field.

Consider the story of Dmitri, a former IT specialist transitioning into sustainable architecture. During his internship at an eco-friendly design firm, he impressed his supervisor with his innovative approach to integrating smart home technology into green building designs. When requesting a recommendation, he specifically asked his supervisor to highlight this unique contribution. The resulting LinkedIn recommendation not only validated Dmitri's technical skills but also showcased his ability to bridge his past expertise with his new passion, catching the eye of several sustainable construction companies.

Timing is crucial when asking for recommendations. Fatima, a volunteer at a local animal shelter transitioning into veterinary medicine, made a point of requesting recommendations immediately after successfully managing a large-scale adoption event. The immediacy allowed her supervisors to provide detailed, enthusiastic endorsements while her contributions were fresh in their minds.

Don't limit yourself to just supervisors. Peer recommendations can also provide valuable insights into your collaborative skills and work ethic. Javier, an aspiring social media manager volunteering for a non-profit, secured a glowing recommendation from a fellow volunteer he had mentored in content creation. This peer endorsement highlighted Javier's leadership and teaching abilities, rounding out his professional profile.

Remember that recommendations on professional networking platforms like LinkedIn are particularly valuable due to their visibility and credibility. Wei, transitioning from academia to data science, made it a priority to secure LinkedIn recommendations from both her internship supervisor and a senior data scientist she had collaborated with on a project. These public endorsements played a crucial role in validating her skills to potential employers who were initially skeptical of her non-traditional background.

Be strategic in your requests. Anika, moving to environmental policy, asked different recommenders to focus on specific aspects of her performance.

She requested her project lead to highlight her research skills while asking the organization's director to comment on her policy analysis abilities. This approach ensured a well-rounded set of recommendations that covered the full spectrum of her newly acquired expertise.

Don't be afraid to provide your recommenders with a brief summary of your contributions and the skills you'd like them to highlight. This not only makes their task easier but also ensures the recommendations align with your career goals. Another person transitioning to corporate training, provided his internship supervisor with a bullet-point list of key projects he had completed, which resulted in a detailed and highly relevant recommendation.

By proactively seeking and strategically managing your recommendations, you're not just collecting praise – you're building a network of professional advocates who can vouch for your abilities in your new field. These endorsements can be the deciding factor that opens doors to exciting opportunities in your new career path.

## The Seal of Approval: The Power of Recommendations

As your internship or volunteer experience draws to a close, getting strong recommendations can be the final piece that completes your career transition puzzle because they serve as testimonials to your newly acquired skills and your potential in your chosen field.

Ivan, a former IT specialist transitioning into sustainable architecture, impressed his supervisor with his innovative approach to integrating smart home technology into green building designs during his internship at an eco-friendly design firm, he. When requesting a recommendation, he specifically asked his supervisor to highlight this contribution. The resulting LinkedIn recommendation not only validated Ivan's technical skills but also showcased his ability to bridge his past expertise with his new passion and caught the eye of several sustainable construction companies.

Timing is crucial when asking for recommendations. Fatima, transitioning into veterinary medicine, made the point of requesting recommendations immediately after successfully managing a large-scale adoption event. The immediacy allowed her supervisors to provide detailed, enthusiastic endorsements while her contributions were fresh in their minds.

Don't limit yourself to supervisors. Peer recommendations can also provide valuable insights into your collaborative skills and work ethic. Javier, an aspiring social media manager volunteering for a non-profit, secured a glowing recommendation from a fellow volunteer he mentored in content creation. This peer endorsement highlighted his leadership and teaching abilities, rounding out his professional profile.

Remember that recommendations on LinkedIn are particularly valuable due to their visibility and credibility. One person made it a priority to get

LinkedIn recommendations from both her internship supervisor and a senior data scientist she had collaborated with on a project. These public endorsements played a crucial role in validating her skills to potential employers who were initially skeptical of her non-traditional background. Be strategic in your requests. Another person asked different people to focus their recommendations on specific aspects of their performance. They asked their project lead to highlight their research skills while asking the organization's director to comment on her policy analysis abilities. This approach ensured a well-rounded set of recommendations that covered the full spectrum of her newly acquired expertise.

Don't be afraid to provide your recommenders with a summary of your contributions and the skills you'd like them to highlight. This not only makes their job easier (remember, you are doing something that may be an inconvenience for them) but also ensures their recommendations align with your career goals.

Omar provided his internship supervisor with a bullet-point list of key projects he had completed, which resulted in a detailed and highly relevant recommendation.

By proactively asking for and strategically managing your recommendations, you're not just collecting praise – you're building a network of professional advocates who can vouch for your abilities in your new field. These endorsements can be the deciding factor that opens doors to exciting opportunities in your new career path.

## Go All In: The Power of Unwavering Commitment

Approaching your volunteer or internship role with unwavering dedication and commitment can set you apart and pave the way for future opportunities. Employers consistently seek individuals who demonstrate passion, proactivity, and a strong work ethic.

Sonia, who transitioned from a career in logistics to marine biology, during her internship at a coastal research station, consistently arrived early to prepare equipment for the day's fieldwork. On one such morning, she noticed an unusual algal bloom near the shore. Her prompt reporting allowed the research team to collect valuable data on an emerging ecological event, leading to a significant publication. Sonia's supervisor later remarked that her dedication and attentiveness had directly contributed to this scientific breakthrough.

Lucas, volunteering at a community theater to gain experience in set design, exemplified commitment by going far above and beyond his assignments. When the lead set builder fell ill a week before opening night, he stepped up, working late into the evenings to ensure the set was completed on time. His efforts not only saved the production but also caught the attention of a visiting director from a larger theater company, who later offered him a paid apprenticeship.

Commitment also means maintaining a positive attitude even during challenging times. One woman faced a major setback when a coding error caused the loss of a week's worth of work. Instead of becoming discouraged, she took the initiative to implement a new version control system, working through the weekend to recover the lost progress. Her resilience and proactive problem-solving impressed the CTO, who subsequently offered her a full-time position.

By approaching every task, no matter how small, with enthusiasm and a commitment to excellence, you demonstrate your value to the organization and set the stage for future success in your new career path.

## From Volunteer to Valued: Navigating the Path to Paid Positions

Exceptional performance during your volunteer or internship experience can be the springboard to paid opportunities, either within the same organization or elsewhere in your new field.

Take the case of Hiroshi, who transitioned from finance to sustainable agriculture. During his volunteer stint at an urban farming initiative, he applied his analytical skills to optimize the farm's crop rotation and resource allocation.

His data-driven approach led to a 30% increase in yield and a significant reduction in water usage. Impressed by these tangible results, the farm's director created a new paid position specifically for him, where he was tasked with implementing his innovative strategies across their network of urban farms.

Esther's journey from volunteering to a paid role in wildlife conservation showcases the importance of networking and visibility. While interning at a national park, she took charge of organizing a community outreach program that successfully engaged local schools in conservation efforts. Her initiative caught the attention of a representative from a larger conservation organization who was visiting the park. Impressed by Esther's passion and results, the representative offered her a paid position coordinating similar programs on a regional scale.

Sometimes, the transition to a paid role requires strategic patience and persistence. Miguel demonstrated his value by streamlining a firm's data management processes. When he inquired about paid positions, he was initially told there were no openings. Undeterred, Miguel proposed a part-time paid role where he would continue his work on data management while also assisting with grant writing. His proposal highlighted the cost savings and increased efficiency his work had already brought to the company. After careful consideration, the startup's management agreed, creating a new hybrid role that allowed Miguel to transition into a paid position.

By consistently delivering exceptional results and demonstrating your value, you position yourself as an indispensable asset, making the transition from volunteer to paid professional a natural progression in your new career path.

Volunteering and interning serve as pivotal stepping stones in your career transition, offering far more than just experience on paper. These opportunities are multifaceted, providing a comprehensive platform for personal and professional growth.

First, they offer a real-world test drive of your new career path. This immersive experience allows you to gauge your genuine interest and aptitude for the field, helping you confirm or recalibrate your career goals. It's an invaluable chance to experience the day-to-day realities of your chosen profession, ensuring that your passion aligns with the practical aspects of the work.

Moreover, these roles serve as a tangible demonstration of your commitment to your new career. They showcase your willingness to invest time and effort into your transition, signaling to potential employers your dedication and seriousness about the change. This commitment can set you apart from other candidates who may lack practical experience in the field.

Volunteering and interning also provide a unique opportunity to contribute meaningfully to organizations or causes aligned with your new career interests. This contribution not only adds value to the organization but also allows you to build a portfolio of real-world accomplishments in your new field.

These experiences are fertile ground for learning and skill development. They offer hands-on training that complements theoretical knowledge, allowing you to develop industry-specific skills and familiarity with relevant tools and practices. This practical knowledge can be invaluable when seeking paid positions in your new field.

Networking is another crucial aspect of these experiences. They provide opportunities to build relationships with professionals in your new field, potentially leading to mentorship, job opportunities, or valuable industry insights. These connections can be instrumental in navigating your career transition.

Furthermore, volunteering and interning allow you to acclimate to the culture and norms of your new industry. This insider perspective can help you adjust your professional persona and communication style to fit your new environment, easing the transition process.

Lastly, these experiences serve as a bridge between your past career and your future aspirations. They provide a space where you can leverage your existing skills while developing new ones, creating a narrative of growth and adaptability that can be compelling to future employers.

In essence, volunteering and interning are not just about gaining experience; they are about holistic professional development. They offer a comprehensive foundation for your career transition, combining practical experience, networking, skill development, and personal growth. This foundation can significantly enhance your readiness and competitiveness as you step into paid roles in your new career path.

# Step 9:

# Mentorship: Your Career Transition Catalyst

Mentorship is more than just a buzzword in career development. It's a transformative force that can catapult your professional journey. When navigating the choppy waters of career transition, having a seasoned navigator by your side can mean the difference between aimless drifting and reaching your desired destination with confidence.

Imagine having access to a living, breathing playbook of industry insights, hard-earned wisdom, and battle-tested strategies. That's what an experienced mentor brings to the table. They've weathered the storms you're about to face, dodged the pitfalls that lie ahead and can illuminate the path forward with the bright light of their experience.

But mentorship isn't a magic wand. It's a dynamic relationship that requires active engagement, clear communication, and a willingness to learn and adapt. When leveraged effectively, it becomes a powerful catalyst for growth, opening doors to opportunities you might never have discovered on your own.

In this section, we'll explore the art of finding, nurturing, and maximizing mentor relationships during your career transition. You'll learn how to identify potential mentors, approach them with purpose, and cultivate meaningful connections that transcend mere professional courtesy. We'll delve into strategies for extracting invaluable insights, translating their advice into actionable steps, and avoiding common mentorship pitfalls.

Remember, the right mentor can compress years of learning into months, helping you leapfrog common obstacles and accelerate your career transformation.

## Identify Potential Mentors

Choosing the right mentor is a critical first step in your career transition. Your ideal mentor should be someone who has not only succeeded in your desired field but also has the insight and empathy to guide others effectively. To identify potential mentors, start by immersing yourself in your target industry. Research industry leaders who have made significant contributions, innovated, or risen to leadership positions. These could be authors of influential books, speakers at industry conferences, or executives at companies you admire.

Don't underestimate the power of professional networks. LinkedIn, for example, can be invaluable for identifying people with career paths that align with your goals. Don't ignore second-degree connections who might be more accessible through mutual contacts. Additionally, industry events such as conferences, workshops, and networking meetups are goldmines for meeting potential mentors. Engage in conversations and keep an eye out for those who seem approachable and passionate about sharing their knowledge.

If you're an alumnus of a college or university, tap into your alumni network. Many successful professionals are eager to give back by mentoring fellow alumni. However, don't limit yourself to obvious choices or "celebrity alumni." Sometimes, the best mentors come from adjacent industries or have taken unconventional paths that could offer unique perspectives on your transition. Consider reaching out to people who have successfully navigated career changes themselves. Their firsthand experience with the challenges and triumphs of transition can be invaluable.

Let's consider an example. Imagine you're a marketing professional looking to transition into the field of data science. Your ideal mentor might be someone who is a Chief Data Officer at a major tech company whose background is particularly relevant because they started their career in marketing, giving them insight into your current skill set and how it can be applied to data science.

They successfully transitioned into data science mid-career, mirroring the journey you're about to undertake. In this example, they regularly speak at industry conferences and have written articles on the intersection of marketing and data science, demonstrating their willingness to share knowledge.

By identifying this person as a potential mentor, you're not just finding someone with technical expertise, but a professional who understands the nuances of career transition in your specific context. This targeted approach to mentor identification increases your chances of forming a meaningful and productive mentorship relationship that can significantly accelerate your career change.

Remember, the goal is to find someone whose experience resonates with your aspirations and who can offer both practical guidance and inspirational leadership as you navigate your career transition. With persistence and a strategic approach, you can identify mentors who will be instrumental in shaping your professional future.

## Weave Your Web: Networking Mastery for Mentor Gold

In the quest for a mentor, your network is your net worth. The art of networking and securing referrals is akin to panning for gold in a river of opportunities. It's about casting your net wide, but with precision, to catch the mentors who can truly elevate your career transition.

Start by tapping into the hidden reservoir of connections that surrounds you. Your professional network is usually more extensive than you initially realize. It's not just about who you know, but who they know. Every colleague, friend, or acquaintance could be the bridge to a great mentor.

Consider the case of Alex, a former teacher trying to break into UX design. Alex began by reaching out to a former classmate who had made a similar transition years ago. While she wasn't in a position to mentor Alex herself, she introduced him to her colleague, Marcus, a seasoned UX designer with a passion for nurturing new talent. This connection, born from a simple catch-up call, blossomed into a mentorship that helped Alex navigate the intricacies of his career shift.

The power of networking extends beyond professional circles. Sometimes, the most valuable connections can be found in unexpected places. Diego was volunteering at a local tech workshop for kids, when he met Olivia, a former software engineer turned successful tech entrepreneur. Their shared passion for education and technology led to a mentorship that helped Diego transition from his role as a high school computer science teacher to a product manager at an edtech startup.

When asking for referrals or introductions, be specific about what you're looking for in a mentor. Instead of a vague request like "Do you know anyone who could mentor me?", try something more targeted: "I'm trying to connect with someone who has successfully transitioned from teaching to tech in the last five years. Do you know anyone who fits that profile?"

Remember, networking for mentorship is a two-way street. As you reach out and connect, think about what you can offer in return. Maybe it's a fresh perspective from your current field, or simply your enthusiasm and willingness to learn. The most rewarding mentorship relationships are those where both parties feel they're gaining something valuable.

By weaving your web of connections with intention and care, you're not just finding a mentor; you're building a support system that can propel your career transition. So, cast your net wide, be bold in your outreach, and watch as the golden opportunities for mentorship begin to shine through. Whether it's through rekindling old connections like Alex did, or forming new ones in unexpected places like Diego, your next great mentor could be just one conversation away.

## Harnessing Professional Organizations

Professional organizations are valuable resources for career transitions, offering numerous opportunities for mentorship. These industry-specific associations serve as hubs where you can connect directly with experienced professionals in your target field.

By joining these organizations, you gain access to a community of professionals who understand the intricacies of the career you're pursuing. These associations often provide industry insights, professional development resources, and opportunities to connect with potential mentors who have experience relevant to your goals.

Many professional organizations offer structured mentorship programs. These programs typically use careful matching processes to pair mentees with mentors whose experiences align with the mentee's objectives. This approach can help you find targeted guidance more efficiently.

Even without formal mentorship programs, these organizations provide opportunities for organic mentor-mentee relationships to develop.

Attending chapter meetings, participating in webinars, or contributing to online forums can help you showcase your interest and potentially attract the attention of experienced professionals willing to offer guidance.

The conferences, workshops, and seminars hosted by these organizations, are excellent venues for meeting potential mentors. Engaging with speakers, participating in discussions, and networking during breaks can lead to valuable connections.

Many organizations also have special interest groups or committees. Volunteering for these groups can put you in contact with industry veterans, allowing you to learn while demonstrating your skills and work ethic. These interactions can sometimes naturally evolve into mentorship relationships.

The digital offerings of these organizations, such as online member directories, discussion boards, and social media groups, can also be useful for identifying potential mentors. Engaging thoughtfully in these spaces by offering insights and asking relevant questions can attract the attention of experienced members.

While membership in professional organizations often requires a fee, consider it an investment in your career transition. The access to resources and potential for mentorship can provide significant benefits.

As you engage with these professional networks, be open to different forms of mentorship. While one-on-one relationships are common, some organizations also facilitate group mentorship sessions or peer mentoring circles, which can offer diverse perspectives.

By actively participating in professional organizations, you position yourself to meet experienced professionals in your desired field. You demonstrate your commitment to the industry and your eagerness to learn, which can make you an attractive candidate for mentorship.

## Using Digital Networks for Mentorship

Online platforms, particularly professional networking sites like LinkedIn, offer practical tools for connecting with potential mentors. These sites provide access to a wide range of experienced professionals across various industries.

When using these platforms, start by refining your search to focus on professionals in your target industry who have the experience and expertise you're seeking. Look for individuals who have successfully navigated career paths similar to the one you're pursuing.

When you identify potential mentors, take the time to craft personalized connection requests. Briefly introduce yourself, explain your career goals, and mention specific aspects of their professional background and expertise that interest you. This targeted approach is more likely to yield positive responses than generic connection requests.

Many professionals on these platforms share thoughts and insights through posts, articles, or comments. Engaging thoughtfully with this content can be an effective way to initiate conversations. Offer meaningful comments or ask insightful questions to demonstrate your genuine interest in their expertise.

Some online platforms offer features specifically designed for mentorship. These might include mentor-matching programs or groups dedicated to career development in specific fields. Explore these options as they can streamline the process of finding suitable mentors.
Remember that building relationships online requires patience and persistence. Not every connection will lead to a mentorship, but each

interaction can provide valuable insights and expand your professional network.

Be mindful of professional etiquette in online spaces. Respect people's time and privacy, and be clear about your intentions when reaching out. If someone agrees to connect, follow up with a thank-you message and, if appropriate, a request for further advice or a brief conversation.

While online platforms can be powerful tools for finding mentors, they work best as part of a broader strategy that includes in-person networking and engagement with professional organizations.

By effectively utilizing these digital networks, you can extend your reach beyond your immediate circle, connecting with experienced professionals who can offer guidance and support as you transition into your new career.

## Crafting Your Mentorship Roadmap

Before embarking on a mentorship quest, get clear about your career transition objective. This self-reflection phase sets the foundation for meaningful mentor relationships.

Start by outlining your specific goals. For instance, Chaim, transitioning to data journalism, might try to understand how to apply his investigative skills to data analysis. His objectives could include learning specific data visualization tools and understanding how to pitch data-driven stories to editors.

Consider what type of guidance would be most beneficial. Ramesh, moving to a startup CFO position, might want a mentor who can provide insights on the unique financial challenges of early-stage companies and advice on building financial systems from the ground up.

Be specific about the areas where you need support. Brooke, shifting from traditional marketing to growth hacking for tech startups, might look for advice on leveraging data analytics for rapid experimentation and scaling user acquisition strategies.

Flexibility is key when considering time commitments. Mentors are often busy professionals offering their time generously. Ellen proposed a monthly video call with her mentor, with the option for occasional email exchanges for quick questions.

Prepare a concise summary of your background, transition goals, and what you hope to gain from the mentorship. This clarity will help potential mentors understand how they can assist you effectively. For example, Tan outlined his classroom experience and expressed his desire to understand how edtech products are developed and implemented.

Remember, mentorship is a two-way street. Consider what you can offer in return. Perhaps your fresh perspective from your previous career could provide valuable insights to your mentor. Brenda, transitioning from social work to human resources, could offer her mentor insights on employee well-being strategies based on her experience in social services.

By approaching potential mentors with well-defined objectives and realistic expectations, you demonstrate respect for their time and increase the likelihood of forming a productive mentorship relationship. This clarity also helps ensure that the guidance you receive aligns closely with your career transition needs.

## Tailor Your Pitch: The Art of Mentor Outreach

When you have your sights set on a potential mentor, it's time to craft an approach that's as unique as your career journey. Think of it as writing a cover letter but with a personal twist.

Kick things off by doing your homework. Dive into their LinkedIn profile, read their articles, or check out any interviews they've given to any form of media. This groundwork will help you connect the dots between their experience and your aspirations.

Now, let's talk about your opening line. Ditch the generic "I'd like to connect" or "I'd like to pick your brain." Go for something that shows you've been paying attention. For example, if you're a project manager eyeing a shift to agile coaching, you might open with, "Your recent article on scaling agile practices in Fortune 500 companies really resonated with me."

Next, give them the rundown on your situation. Keep it brief, but paint a clear picture. "I'm currently transitioning from traditional project management to agile coaching, and your evolution from team lead to agile transformation consultant caught my eye."

Here's where you can make it personal. Highlight something specific about their career that inspires you. Maybe it's a particular achievement or a unique approach they've taken. "Your success in helping non-tech companies adopt agile methodologies is exactly the kind of impact I hope to make in my new role."

Don't forget to explain why you think they'd be a great mentor for you. Is it their industry experience? Their leadership style? Their innovative approach? Spell it out. "Your experience bridging the gap between traditional and agile methodologies is incredibly relevant to my circumstances, and I believe your insights would be invaluable."

Wrap it up by being clear about what you're asking for, but keep it low-pressure. "I'd love the opportunity to have a 20-minute call to discuss your experiences and any advice you might have for someone in my position. Of course, I understand if your schedule doesn't permit, and I appreciate your time either way."

Remember, the goal here is to show that you're thoughtful, prepared, and genuinely interested in their specific experiences and insights. By personalizing your approach, you're not just another name in their inbox – you're a potential mentee who's done their homework and is ready to learn.

## Give and Take: Two-Way Mentorship

Mentorship is not just about you soaking up all that wisdom - it's about creating a relationship where both of you get something valuable out of the deal.

First off, ditch the idea that you're just a sponge here to absorb knowledge. Sure, you're looking to learn, but you've got plenty to bring to the table too. Maybe you're a whiz with social media and your potential mentor's LinkedIn profile could use a facelift. Perhaps your fresh perspective from your current field could offer a few creative solutions to their industry challenges.

When you're reaching out, don't be shy about highlighting what you can offer. For example, "While I'd love to learn from your experience in fintech, I'd be happy to share insights from my background in behavioral economics that might add a unique perspective to your customer acquisition strategies."

Be open to rolling up your sleeves and putting in some work. If your mentor mentions a project they're working on, don't be afraid to say, " I'd love to help out if you need an extra pair of hands." This shows you're not just in it for the quick advice - you're willing to invest time and effort into the relationship.

Remember, mentors often get a kick out of seeing their proteges succeed. Your progress and achievements can be incredibly rewarding for them. So, keep them in the loop about how you're applying their advice and the wins you're scoring along the way.

And here's a pro tip: sometimes, the best way to give back is simply to be an awesome mentee. Show up prepared for your conversations, follow through on their suggestions, and let them know how their advice is making a difference. Trust me, for many mentors, seeing you crush your goals is the best return on investment they could ask for.

The bottom line is to approach mentorship like a partnership, not a one-way street. Be proactive, be generous with your skills and time, and always be on the lookout for ways to add value to them. That's how you turn a mentorship into a long-lasting, mutually beneficial relationship.

## Charting Your Mentorship Course

Alright, you've landed a mentor! Now it's time to get down to brass tacks and map out what this mentorship journey will look like.

Let's talk goals. What are you aiming for here? Maybe you're looking to switch gears in your career and need some insider knowledge, or you're eyeing that corner office and want tips on climbing the corporate ladder. Whatever it is, lay it all out on the table.

Next up, let's figure out the nuts and bolts of how this is going to work. How often are you going to touch base? Are we talking weekly coffee chats, monthly video calls, or just firing off emails when you need a quick dose of wisdom? Remember, your mentor's probably juggling a packed schedule, so find a rhythm that works for both of you.

Don't forget to nail down your preferred communication channels. Are you a face-to-face kind of person, or is Slack more your speed? Getting this sorted upfront can save a lot of back-and-forth later.

Lastly, zero in on the areas you really want to focus on. Maybe it's beefing up your networking skills or getting the inside scoop on industry trends. Being specific here will help your mentor tailor their advice to what you really need.

Remember, setting expectations isn't about boxing yourself in - it's about creating a roadmap that'll help both of you get the most out of this mentorship. With everyone on the same page, you can dive into the good stuff: learning, growing, and hopefully having some fun along the way.

## Define Your Mentorship: Set Clear Expectations

Once you have a mentor, it's time to establish a clear framework for your relationship. Think of this as laying the groundwork for a productive and rewarding mentorship experience.

Start by explaining your goals. What do you hope to achieve through mentorship? Maybe you're aiming for a career transition and need industry insights, or you're targeting a leadership role and want guidance on developing essential skills. Be specific about your objectives to help your mentor understand how they can best support you.

Next, discuss the logistics of your interactions. How frequently will you meet? Will it be in person, via video calls, or email exchanges? Consider your mentor's schedule and find a rhythm that works for both of you. It's important to balance between regular contact and respecting their time commitments.

Agree on your preferred communication channels. Whether it's face-to-face meetings, video conferences, or a mix of methods, establishing this upfront will streamline your interactions and set clear expectations for both of you.

Finally, identify the specific areas you want to focus on during your mentorship. This might include developing particular skills, understanding industry trends, or navigating career challenges. Being clear will help your mentor tailor their guidance to your wants and needs.

Remember, setting expectations isn't about creating rigid rules, but about establishing a flexible structure that allows both of you to get the most out of this mentorship. With a clear understanding in place, you can concentrate on the valuable process of learning, growing, and advancing your career goals.

## Learn and Maximize Your Mentorship

Approach each interaction with your mentor as a valuable learning opportunity. Your active engagement won't only enhance your growth but also make the experience more rewarding for your mentor.

Ask thoughtful questions that demonstrate your curiosity and commitment. For example, if your mentor shares a strategy they used to overcome a career challenge, you might ask, "How did you adapt that approach for different situations?" or "What were some unexpected outcomes of using that strategy?"

Ask for specific guidance on your current challenges. If you're struggling with a particular aspect of your transition, don't hesitate to bring it up. For instance, "I'm finding it difficult to translate my skills from marketing to data analysis. How would you suggest I bridge this gap?"

Actively apply the advice you receive. If your mentor suggests a new approach or resource, try it out before your next meeting. Then, share your experience: "I implemented the networking strategy you recommended at last week's industry event. Here's what worked well and where I struggled..."

Take notes during your conversations. This shows respect for your mentor's time and helps you retain important insights. You might say, "I've been jotting down key points from our discussions. Your advice on negotiating job offers has been particularly helpful."

Share your progress and setbacks. Your mentor will appreciate knowing how their guidance is impacting your journey. For example, "Following your advice, I have three informational interviews in my target industry. However, I'm still nervous about how to make the most of these opportunities."

Don't be afraid to respectfully challenge ideas or seek clarification. If something doesn't align with your experience or understanding, discuss it. You might say, "That approach seems different from what I've read about the industry. Could you help me understand why it might be more effective?"

Consider sharing relevant articles or industry news with your mentor to spark discussions. This shows initiative and can lead to valuable conversations: "I came across this article about emerging trends in our field. I'd love to get your perspective on how this might affect career opportunities."

Remember, active learning isn't just about absorbing information—it's about engaging with it, applying it, and reflecting on the results. By doing so, you'll make the most of your mentorship and demonstrate your commitment to growth.

## Fuel Your Growth with Feedback and Accountability

Embrace feedback and accountability as drivers of your career transition. A good mentor will challenge you, pushing you beyond your comfort to accelerate your growth.

Actively ask for constructive feedback. After presenting your ideas or sharing your progress, you might ask, "What areas do you think I need to improve?" or "How could I have approached this situation more effectively?" This openness to critique demonstrates your commitment to growth.

Sarah was actively transitioning to UX design when her mentor suggested she create a portfolio of sample projects. When Sarah presented her work, her mentor pointed out that while her designs were visually appealing, they lacked user research backing. This feedback helped Sarah refocus her efforts on the user-centered aspects of UX design.

Set measurable goals and share them with your mentor. For instance, "By next month, I will complete two online courses in data analysis and apply for three entry-level positions in the field." This gives your mentor concrete benchmarks to help you track your progress.

Welcome challenges from your mentor. When Alex was transitioning to corporate training, he expressed doubt about his ability to adapt to a business environment. His mentor challenged him to lead a training session for a local business group. This push helped Alex realize how transferable his skills were.

Be proactive about accountability. You might say, "Could we start each session with a brief review of the goals we set last time?" This shows you're serious about making progress and that you value your mentor's time.

Share both successes and setbacks. When Mia landed her first consulting gig, she immediately informed her mentor. But she also reached out when she struggled with a particularly complex project, allowing her mentor to provide timely guidance.

Ask your mentor to point out blind spots. Rob, moving from journalism to public relations, was surprised when his mentor highlighted his habit of burying the lead in press releases – a habit from his long-form writing days. This insight helped Rob adapt his writing style quickly.

Remember, constructive feedback and accountability aren't about criticism – they're tools for improvement. By embracing them, you're demonstrating your commitment to your career transition and making the most of your mentor's expertise.

## Keep Up the Momentum with Regular Check-Ins

Consistent communication with your mentor is crucial for maintaining momentum. Regular check-ins provide opportunities for guidance, support, and course correction.

Establish a rhythm for your updates. You might suggest, "Could we have a brief catch-up every two weeks? I'd like to share my progress and get your input on any challenges I'm facing."

For example, Lena, transitioning to data analytics, set up bi-weekly video calls with her mentor. During these sessions, she'd share her progress on learning Python and discuss any roadblocks she encountered in her job search.

Be proactive in your communications. Don't wait for your mentor to ask – volunteer information about your journey. You could say, "I wanted to let you know that I've completed the cybersecurity certification we discussed. I'm now looking at how to leverage this in my job applications."

Kai, moving from teaching to instructional design, made it a habit to email his mentor a brief summary of his weekly activities and any questions he had. This kept his mentor in the loop and allowed for timely advice.

Share both victories and setbacks. When Yasmin was transitioning to human resources, and completed her first employment law course, she immediately informed her mentor. But she also reached out when she struggled with a particularly challenging interview, allowing her mentor to provide timely support and strategies.

Use these check-ins to seek specific advice. When Omar was shifting from civil engineering to sustainable urban planning, he would prepare questions for each meeting. For instance, "I've noticed a trend towards green infrastructure in job postings. How can I best highlight my transferable skills in this area?"

Don't forget to update your mentor on how you've applied their previous advice. You might say, "Remember that networking strategy you suggested? I've been using it at industry events, and it's already led to two informational interviews."

Be open about possible changes in your goals based on events and circumstances. Noticing an unexpected interest can lead to a fruitful discussion this shift that refocuses your transition strategy.

Remember, regular check-ins aren't just about reporting – they're opportunities for learning, adjustment, and growth. By keeping your mentor informed and engaged, you're maximizing the value of their guidance and demonstrating your commitment to your career transition.

## Mentor Mixology: Blending Voices for Career Success

Embracing multiple mentors or advisors can enrich your career transition by offering a kaleidoscope of insights and guidance. Think of it as assembling a personal board of directors for your career.

Seek out mentors from various backgrounds and areas of expertise. For example, you might have one mentor who's an industry veteran, another who is a recent career changer, and a third who excels in a specific skill you're trying to develop.

For instance, Noah, transitioning from traditional marketing to growth hacking, cultivated relationships with three mentors: a seasoned growth hacker, a data analyst, and a startup founder. This trio provided him with technical know-how, analytical skills, and entrepreneurial insights respectively.

Don't limit yourself to mentors within your target industry. Erica, switching to corporate communications, found great guidance from a theater director on storytelling and presentation skills - abilities crucial in her new field.

Consider mentors at different career stages. Nadia, shifting from corporate law to non-profit management, benefited from the perspectives of both a non-profit CEO and a program coordinator who had recently made a similar transition.

Leverage your mentors' strengths. You might turn to one for strategic career advice, another for technical skills development, and a third for networking opportunities.

Be clear with each mentor about their role. You could say, "I really value your expertise in project management. Would you be open to focusing our discussions on how I can apply these skills in my transition to product management?"

Cross-pollinate ideas between your mentors. Share insights you've gained from one mentor with another to get different perspectives. For example, "My mentor in fintech suggested I focus on blockchain technologies. What's your take on this, given your experience in traditional banking?"

Remember to manage these relationships carefully. As always, be respectful of each mentor's time and be clear about your interactions with other mentors to avoid any sense of competition.

By cultivating a diverse mentorship network, you're creating a robust support system that can guide you through various aspects of your career transition. This multifaceted approach can lead to more comprehensive growth and open up unexpected opportunities along your journey.

## Be Mindful and Considerate: The Art of Respectful Guidance

Respecting your mentor's time and boundaries is crucial for maintaining a healthy, productive mentorship. Remember, your mentor is likely balancing multiple responsibilities alongside their commitment to you. They are giving of themselves to help you at the price of time at work or with friends and family.

Be mindful of your mentor's schedule. When arranging meetings, you might say, "I understand you have a busy schedule. Would it be convenient to meet for 30 minutes next week? I'm happy to work around your availability."

In Tasha's switch to corporate training, she always came prepared with a focused agenda for her mentor meetings. This approach ensured they made the most of their limited time together and demonstrated her respect for her mentor's busy executive schedule.

Be flexible and understanding if your mentor needs to reschedule. After all, your mentor has a life and a career beyond supporting you. One of the things that made your mentor attractive to you was their success and character. Occasionally, those responsibilities will cause them to postpone their calls due to urgent work matters. Instead of feeling discouraged, use these instances to practice adaptability - a crucial skill in a new field.

Respect communication preferences. Some mentors might prefer email updates, while others may be more responsive to brief texts or calls. You may discover your mentor prefers text messages for quick questions and saved longer discussions for their bi-weekly video calls.

Be thoughtful about the frequency of your contact. Unless agreed otherwise, avoid bombarding your mentor with daily updates or questions. Consider making a rule to compile your questions and insights into a weekly email, which your mentor can respond to efficiently.

Understand that your mentor's guidance has limits. When Simone faced a challenging project, her mentor offered valuable advice but made it clear that she needed to make the final decisions herself. This boundary helped her develop crucial problem-solving skills.

Show appreciation for your mentor's time and efforts. After a particularly insightful session, send a brief thank-you note highlighting the specific advice that you found most valuable.

Be aware of the mentorship's scope. You might find you need a specific technical training your mentor can't provide, look for additional resources while maintaining the valuable strategic guidance from your mentor.

Remember, respecting boundaries isn't about limiting your growth - it's about fostering a sustainable, mutually beneficial mentorship. By showing consideration for your mentor's time and limits, you're more likely to build a lasting relationship that continues to support your career transition and beyond.

## Gratitude Amplified: Fuel Your Mentorship with Appreciation

Expressing gratitude isn't just good manners—it's the secret sauce that can transform a good mentorship into a great one. Your mentor is investing their time, knowledge, and energy in your growth. Acknowledging this investment can deepen your relationship and motivate your mentor to continue their support.

Start with the basics: a sincere "thank you" at the end of each session. But don't stop there. Be specific about what you're grateful for. Instead of a generic "thanks for your help," try "I really appreciate how you broke down that complex industry concept for me. It's made a significant difference in my understanding."

Consider sending a thoughtful email after particularly insightful sessions. Highlight the key takeaways and how you plan to apply them. This not only shows gratitude but also demonstrates that you're actively engaging with their advice.

Periodically reflect on your progress and share it with your mentor. Let them know how their guidance has contributed to your growth. Small gestures can speak volumes. If your mentor mentions a book they love, consider reading it and sharing your thoughts. This shows you value their recommendations and are eager to learn.

During your career transition, keep your mentor updated on significant milestones. Let them know whether it's completing a relevant course, securing an informational interview, or landing a new role. Their investment in you makes your successes their successes, too.

If appropriate, offer to help your mentor in return. Perhaps you have skills or connections that could be useful to them. This reciprocity can evolve your relationship into a more collaborative partnership. Remember, they may not ask but if you listen carefully, you may hear opportunities to support them as they've helped you.

Consider tangible tokens of appreciation, but keep them modest and meaningful. A handwritten note, a relevant article you think they'd enjoy, or a small donation to a cause they care about can be touching gestures. Remember, the most sincere form of gratitude is applying their advice and making progress in your career transition. Your success and growth are the ultimate "thank you" to a dedicated mentor.

By consistently expressing your appreciation, you're not just being polite—you're nurturing a relationship that can continue to support and inspire you long after your initial career transition is complete.

## Leverage Mentors for Career Metamorphosis

Mentorship is more than just a buzzword in career development—it's a powerful engine that can turbocharge your professional metamorphosis. As you navigate the complex terrain of career transition, a mentor serves as your experienced guide, map, and compass all rolled into one.

Think of mentorship as your fast-track to success in your new field. It's like having access to a cheat code in a video game, allowing you to bypass obstacles that might otherwise slow you down or derail your progress entirely. A mentor's insights can help you leapfrog over common mistakes, saving you time, energy, and potential career setbacks.

But mentorship goes beyond mere advice-giving. It's a dynamic, evolving relationship that adapts to your needs as you progress through your career transition. Your mentor becomes a sounding board for your ideas, helping you refine your thoughts and strategies. They challenge your assumptions, push you out of your comfort zone, and encourage you to think bigger and bolder about your career possibilities.

One of the most valuable aspects of mentorship is the access it provides to your new industry's inner workings. Your mentor can offer a behind-the-scenes look at your target field, sharing unwritten rules, industry trends, and cultural nuances that you might not discover on your own. This insider knowledge can be invaluable as you position yourself for success in your new career.

Moreover, a good mentor opens doors to their professional network, connecting you with key players in your new field. These connections can lead to informational interviews, job opportunities, or even partnerships that might have been out of reach otherwise. After all, your mentor lends you their professional credibility, helping you establish yourself more quickly in your new industry.

Mentorship also provides a crucial support system during what can be a challenging and sometimes uncertain process. Career transitions often come with moments of doubt or frustration. Your mentor can offer perspective, encouragement, and reassurance, helping you maintain momentum even when the going gets tough.

Remember, the impact of mentorship extends far beyond your immediate career transition. The lessons learned, skills developed, and relationships formed through this process can continue to benefit you throughout your professional life. Many mentees find that they carry the wisdom gained from their mentors for years to come, applying it to future challenges and opportunities.

In essence, mentorship is not just a nice-to-have in your career transition toolkit—it's a must-have. It's an investment in your professional future that can yield returns far beyond your initial career change. By accelerating your learning, expanding your network, and providing crucial support, mentorship can be the difference between a good career transition and a great one.

So, as you embark on your career change journey, make finding and nurturing a mentorship relationship a top priority. It could be the decision that, not only eases your transition, but propels you to heights in your new career that you never thought possible.

# Step 10:

# Unlocking Career Doors Through Professional Associations

In the labyrinth of career transitions, professional associations serve as a trusty compass and roadmap rolled into one. These organizations are more than just fancy letterheads on your resume; they're another ticket to the inner circle of your desired industry, field or work.

Like having a backstage pass to the concert of your dreams, joining professional associations feels like that when you're pivoting careers. It's where the industry's movers and shakers gather, where cutting-edge ideas are born, and where opportunities lurk around every corner.

But here's the kicker: professional associations aren't just about rubbing elbows with leaders. They're about arming yourself with knowledge, skills, and connections that can transform you from an industry outsider to an insider practically overnight.

From webinars that keep you up-to-date with the pulse of trends to mentorship programs that pair you with seasoned pros, these associations are frequently a career changer's secret weapon. They offer a smorgasbord of resources designed to fast-track your transition and give you the insider edge that job boards and LinkedIn can't match.

**Hunt, Hustle, Connect: Zeroing in on Your Career Tribe**

Unearthing the right professional associations is like striking gold in your career transition journey. It's an important step that requires strategic thinking and research. To become a pro at identifying the associations that may catapult your career change, start by immersing yourself in your target industry's landscape. Scan trade publications, industry blogs, and news sites for mentions of prominent organizations, looking for recurring names that pop up in industry discussions and events.

Your digital detective work should involve leveraging search engines with targeted queries like "[Your field] professional association" or "[Industry] organizations." Explore professional networking sites, particularly LinkedIn, for groups and organizations in your desired field, and check out online directories such as CareerOneStop's professional association finder to locate those specifically designed for your industry. Google "What online directories will help me find professional associations?"

Don't overlook academia as a valuable resource. Reach out to universities offering programs in your target field. Many departments maintain lists of relevant professional organizations for their students and alumni. Tap into your existing network, including former colleagues, mentors, or alumni associations, and ask for recommendations on reputable organizations in your desired industry.

Examining the profiles of professionals already working in your target roles can provide valuable clues. Note any associations they're members of or mention. Consider the geographical reach that aligns with your career goals; local chapters might offer more intimate networking opportunities and information about jobs and careers in your local area while national or international organizations could provide broader industry exposure and resources.

Look for specialized associations that cater to specific sub-sectors or roles within your target industry. These niche groups often offer more targeted networking and learning opportunities. Government websites related to your industry can be a goldmine for lists of recognized professional bodies, particularly useful for regulated professions.

Research major conferences or trade shows in your target industry. The organizations hosting or prominently featured at these events are often key players in the field. Don't forget to leverage social media by following industry hashtags on platforms like Twitter or Instagram. Professional associations often have an active social media presence, making them easier to discover.

Remember, the goal isn't to join every association you come across. It's about finding the ones that align most closely with your career transition goals and offer the most valuable resources and connections for your unique needs. Quality trumps quantity every time in this quest for your professional tribe. By employing these varied approaches, you'll be well on your way to identifying the associations that can truly make a difference in your career transition.

## Unlocking the Treasure Trove: Decoding Association Perks

Each organization offers a unique blend of advantages, and it's important to scrutinize these offerings with the precision of a jeweler examining precious gems.

Start by dissecting the association's knowledge base. Many provide exclusive access to cutting-edge industry publications, research reports, and whitepapers that can transform you into a well-informed insider. These resources often come at a premium for non-members, making your membership an instant ticket to insider intelligence.

Next, explore the association's event calendar. High-caliber conferences and networking events can be gold mines for connection-building and learning. These gatherings often feature thought leaders and decision-makers, offering you the chance to engage with the industry's elite. Virtual or in-person, these events can be catalysts for your career transition.

Continuing education is another cornerstone of membership value. Dive into the professional development opportunities offered. From skill-building webinars to certification programs, these learning opportunities can bolster your credentials and close skill gaps as you pivot into your new field.

Some will have job boards. Many associations curate job listings that never appear on public platforms, giving you a competitive edge in your job search. Some even offer career counseling services or resume review sessions tailored to your industry.

Mentorship programs are another invaluable benefit to watch for. The opportunity to be guided by a seasoned professional in your target field can provide insights and shortcuts that could take years to acquire on your own.

Some associations offer tiered pricing based on career stage or income level, which can be a boon for career changers. Others might have introductory rates or trial periods, allowing you to test the waters before diving in fully. Don't forget to factor in any potential tax deductions for professional memberships in your calculations.

Evaluate the time commitment required to leverage the membership benefits. Will you have the bandwidth to attend monthly meetings, participate in committees, or engage in online forums? The most valuable membership is one you can fully utilize.

Align these costs with your career transition timeline and goals. A higher-priced membership might be justifiable if it offers direct access to decision-makers in your target industry or exclusive job placement services. Conversely, a more affordable option might be the smarter choice if you're still in the exploratory phase of your career change.

Don't shy away from reaching out to the association directly to discuss your situation. Some will offer flexibility or special considerations for career transitioners, such as installment payment plans or reduced rates for those between jobs.

Lastly, consider the intangible benefits. Many associations offer members-only online forums or communities where you can engage in discussions, seek advice, and build relationships with peers and leaders in your new field.

The right association membership can yield dividends in the form of knowledge, connections, and opportunities that far outweigh the initial outlay. By meticulously evaluating benefits, you can determine which offers the best mix of resources to fuel your career transition. Remember, the right membership can be a powerful catalyst, accelerating your journey from industry newcomer to established professional.

# Global Reach, Local Touch: Maximizing Your Association Footprint

Often, professional associations have a dual structure of local chapters nested within larger national or international organizations. This tiered approach offers a rich tapestry of opportunities for career transitioners, each level providing unique benefits that can significantly boost your professional metamorphosis.

Typically, local chapters are the grassroots of professional associations, offering an intimate, community-centric experience. These smaller units will usually host regular meetups, workshops, and networking events in your immediate area. The beauty of local involvement lies in its accessibility and frequency. You might find yourself at monthly happy hours, quarterly seminars, or annual conferences, all without the need for extensive travel.

The value of these local connections can't be overstated. They provide a platform to build face-to-face relationships with professionals in your target industry who understand the nuances of the local job market. These connections can lead to mentorship opportunities, insider job leads, and a support network of peers who have or are navigating similar career paths.

On the flip side, national or international associations cast a wider net, offering a broader perspective and more extensive resources. These larger bodies often spearhead industry-wide initiatives, conduct large-scale research, and host major conferences that attract top-tier speakers and attendees from across the globe. Membership at this level can grant you access to job boards, extensive online learning platforms, and certification programs that carry weight across the industry.

The synergy between local and national membership can be powerful. While your local chapter keeps you grounded in your local professional community, the national association provides a bird's-eye view of industry trends, technological advancements, and global opportunities. This dual membership approach allows you to simultaneously think globally and act locally in your career transition strategy.

Consider how this two-pronged approach aligns with your career goals. If you're looking to make a local impact or transition within your current geographical area, heavy involvement in your local chapter might be the priority. If your ambitions include relocating or working for multinational organizations, leaning into the resources of the national or international body could be more beneficial. Remember, you can always ask for advice for people in your local chapter or simply start locally, learn what is available and then escalate to national membership.

Don't overlook the potential for leadership opportunities at both levels. Local chapters often have a more accessible path to committee or board positions, allowing you to quickly build your reputation and skillset. National associations, while more competitive, can offer high-profile volunteer roles that significantly boost your industry visibility.

Remember, many national associations offer bundled memberships that include local chapter access, providing a comprehensive package that covers all bases. This can be a cost-effective way to maximize your exposure and opportunities.

By engaging with both local and national chapters, you can create a multi-dimensional network that supports your career transition from all angles. This approach ensures you're well-connected on the ground while staying attuned to the broader currents shaping your new industry, positioning you for success in your evolving career landscape.

## Master the Conference Circuit

Professional association events and conferences are not just gatherings but career-changing opportunities disguised as social occasions. These assemblies serve as microcosms of your target industry, condensing years of networking and learning into intense, opportunity-rich days.

The spectrum of events is vast, ranging from intimate local meetups to sprawling international conferences. Each type offers unique advantages for the savvy career transitioner. Local events, such as breakfast seminars or after-work mixers, provide frequent touchpoints with your immediate professional community. These smaller-scale gatherings often foster deeper connections and can be easier to navigate for those new to the industry.

On a grander scale, annual conferences are the crown jewels of association events. These multi-day extravaganzas are an array of career advancement opportunities. Keynote speeches from industry luminaries offer glimpses into future trends and big-picture thinking. Breakout sessions dive deep into specific topics, allowing you to build expertise in niche areas of your new field rapidly.

The exhibition halls at these conferences are treasure troves of information and connections. Here, you can directly engage with vendors, potential employers, and industry innovators. It's an unparalleled opportunity to get hands-on with the latest technologies, products, and services shaping your new field.

Networking at these events is an art form unto itself. Beyond the scheduled sessions, informal gatherings like coffee breaks, lunch tables, and evening receptions are where the magic often happens. These are the moments where you can strike up conversations with peers, mentors, and even potential employers in a relaxed setting.

**To maximize your conference experience:**

1. Review the agenda beforehand and plan your schedule strategically.

2. Prepare an elevator pitch that explains your career transition and goals. You can find a great model for one at JobSearch.Community in a free video

3. Set specific networking goals for each day.

4. Actively participate in sessions and conversations by asking thoughtful questions.

5. Follow up with new connections promptly after the event. Have a shareable contact card in your phone that you can send to someone. Ask them to do the same for you.

6. If they don't have one set up, hand them your phone and ask them to enter their contact information into it.

Many associations now offer virtual or hybrid event options, making attendance more accessible. While these lack the in-person energy, they still provide valuable learning and networking opportunities, often with the added benefit of recorded sessions you can revisit.

Beyond attending, consider how you might contribute to these events. Volunteering at a conference can provide behind-the-scenes access and unique networking opportunities. As you build expertise in your new field, you might even propose speaking at an event, establishing yourself as a thought leader in your new industry.

Remember, the true value of these events extends far beyond the days of the gathering itself. The connections made, knowledge gained, and inspiration sparked can fuel your career transition for months or even years to come. By fully embracing the event and conference offerings of your chosen associations, you're not just attending gatherings – you're positioning yourself at the heart of your new profession.

## Harnessing an Association's Online Resources

Many professional associations have transformed their online presence into robust ecosystems of career advancement tools. These websites are no longer mere appendages to physical memberships but have become powerful engines of professional growth in their own right.

At the forefront of these digital offerings are webinars, the new foundation of professional education. These online seminars cover a variety of topics, from broad industry trends to niche technical skills. The beauty of webinars lies in their accessibility and flexibility. You can often attend live sessions and engage directly with presenters through Q&A, or access recordings at your convenience. This allows you to curate a personalized learning path that fits your schedule and specific career transition needs.

Forums and online communities hosted by associations are digital watering holes where industry professionals congregate. These platforms offer unparalleled opportunities to tap into the collective wisdom of your new field. Here, you can pose questions, share insights, and engage in discussions that range from practical job-seeking advice to deep dives into industry challenges. The asynchronous nature of these forums means you can engage in meaningful professional discourse around the clock, expanding your network beyond geographical and time zone constraints.

Industry-specific publications, often available in digital formats, serve as your window into the pulse of your new field. These might include e-magazines, newsletters, or comprehensive research reports. Regular engagement with these publications keeps you informed about industry developments, emerging trends, and potential disruptions. This knowledge is invaluable in interviews and networking situations, allowing you to speak authoritatively about current industry issues.

Many associations also offer digital libraries or resource centers. These repositories can include white papers, case studies, and best practice guides. For a career transitioner, these resources are akin to a shortcut to industry expertise, helping you quickly get up to speed on key concepts and methodologies in your new field.

Online job boards curated by professional associations are often treasure troves of opportunities. Unlike general job sites, these platforms typically feature positions that are highly relevant to your target industry, sometimes including exclusive listings not found elsewhere.

Virtual mentoring programs are another digital gem offered by many associations. These platforms match you with experienced professionals in your desired field, facilitating guidance and support that can be crucial during a career transition.

To maximize these online resources:

1. Create a schedule for regular engagement with online content.

2. Set up alerts for new webinars or publications in areas of particular interest.

3. Actively participate in forum discussions, positioning yourself as a thoughtful contributor.

4. Use the knowledge gained from these resources to inform your networking and interview talking points.

5. Leverage digital platforms to build your personal brand within the industry.

Remember, the key to extracting value from these online resources is consistent, purposeful engagement. By immersing yourself in these digital offerings, you're not just consuming information; you're actively participating in the professional discourse of your new industry. This engagement can accelerate your learning curve, expand your professional network, and position you as an engaged, knowledgeable candidate in your new field.

In the landscape of career transitions, these online resources are not just supplementary – they're essential tools that can significantly flatten the learning curve and open doors in your new professional realm.

## Transform Contacts into Career Gold

Networking within professional associations is a way to catapult your career transition from aspiration to reality. These organizations are not just groups; they're ecosystems teeming with potential mentors, collaborators, and future colleagues. Mastering the art of association networking can be the difference between a sluggish career change and a meteoric rise in your new field.

Association events are fertile ground for beginning relationships and building relationships. From casual mixer nights to formal galas, each gathering is an opportunity to weave yourself into the fabric of your new industry. Approach them with a strategy.

Before attending, research key attendees or speakers, prepare thoughtful questions, and craft an engaging elevator pitch that succinctly conveys your transition story and aspirations.

The key to successful networking at these events is authenticity coupled with curiosity. Instead of approaching conversations with a selfish "what can I get" mindset, focus on "what can I learn." This genuine interest in others' experiences and insights not only makes for more meaningful connections but also positions you as a thoughtful, engaged professional.

Don't underestimate the power of association committees or special interest groups. Volunteering for these smaller units within the larger association provides a dual benefit: it allows you to contribute your skills (even those from your previous career) while working closely with established professionals in your new field. This proximity can lead to organic mentorship relationships and insider knowledge of job opportunities.

Online forums and digital networking platforms provided by associations are extensions of these in-person opportunities. Engage regularly in these spaces, offering insights where you can and asking thoughtful questions. Consistency in these digital spaces can build your reputation as an active, knowledgeable member of the community.

As I've said, association mentorship programs are gold mines for career transitioners. These structured relationships can provide you with a roadmap for your transition, insider advice on industry nuances, and potentially, introductions to key players in your new field. Be proactive in seeking out and nurturing these mentorship opportunities.

Remember, effective networking is a two-way street. Always be on the lookout for ways you can add value, whether it's sharing an interesting article, making an introduction, or offering skills from your previous career that might be valuable in your new industry context.

Follow-up is crucial in turning fleeting event interactions into lasting professional relationships. Develop a system for recording key details about new contacts and following up promptly with personalized messages. Reference specific conversation points and suggest concrete next steps for staying in touch.

Leverage the association's events calendar to create a networking strategy. Try to attend a mix of educational and social events, ensuring a balanced approach to building both your knowledge and your professional network. As you become more established in the association, consider taking on leadership roles or presenting at events. These high-visibility positions can rapidly accelerate your integration into the industry and expand your network exponentially.

Lastly, patience and persistence are key. Building a robust professional network takes time, especially when transitioning careers. Consistently show up, engage genuinely, and focus on building long-term relationships rather than quick wins.

By fully embracing the networking opportunities within professional associations, you're not just collecting contacts ion your phone or business cards; you're cultivating a support system, a knowledge network, and a launchpad for your new career. Each connection made is a potential turning point in your professional journey, a chance to transform a casual conversation into a career-changing opportunity.

## Climbing the Association Ladder

Volunteering for leadership roles within professional associations is a strategic move that can rapidly elevate your profile, expand your network, and provide invaluable industry experience.

Sarah, trying to break into corporate training, joined her local Association for Talent Development chapter. She initially felt overwhelmed and out of place. However, she noticed the chapter was struggling with their social media presence - an area where she had developed. Sarah volunteered to help manage the chapter's social media accounts. Within months, she was not only boosting the chapter's online engagement but also connecting with learning and development professionals across the country. Her visibility within the association skyrocketed, leading to job offers from companies who noticed her knack for digital communication and adult learning principles.

Leadership roles in associations come in various forms, each offering unique benefits:

1. **Committee Membership:** Joining a committee is often the first step on the leadership ladder. It provides insight into the association's inner workings and allows you to contribute your skills in a focused area.

2. **Event Planning:** Organizing conferences or workshops puts you in direct contact with industry speakers and sponsors, expanding your network exponentially.

3. Mentorship Programs: Coordinating mentorship initiatives not only helps others but also positions you as a connector.

4. **Board Positions:** Serving on the board offers high-level strategic experience and unparalleled networking opportunities.

Monroe, a software developer transitioning to cybersecurity, joined the Information Systems Security Association (ISSA) and volunteered to help organize their annual conference. This role required him to reach out to potential speakers - many of whom were leading figures in cybersecurity. Through these interactions, he not only learned about trends but also formed relationships with key industry players. One of these connections eventually led to a job offer that kickstarted his cybersecurity career.

The beauty of volunteer leadership roles is that they help you to demonstrate skills and gain experience directly relevant to your new field. For instance, Emma wanted to move into marketing. She took on the role of newsletter editor for her marketing association. This position allowed her to showcase her writing and editing skills in a marketing context, making her transition much smoother when applying for content marketing positions.

It's crucial to approach these roles with genuine commitment and enthusiasm. One woman I know learned this lesson the hard way when she hastily volunteered for a board position with a local charitable organization. Initially viewing it as merely a resume booster, she quickly realized the depth of responsibility involved. Her commitment wavered, affecting her reputation within the organization. This underscores the importance of choosing roles that align not just with your career goals, but also with your passions and available time.

## When considering leadership roles:

1. **Start small and grow:** Begin with manageable commitments and gradually take on more responsibility.

2. **Align with your goals:** Choose roles that develop skills or provide experiences relevant to your target career.

3. **Be reliable:** Consistent, quality contributions build your reputation quickly.

4. **Network strategically:** Use your position to form meaningful connections with industry leaders.

5. **Seek mentorship:** Many associations pair new leaders with experienced members, providing invaluable guidance.

Remember, leadership roles in associations are not just about adding a line to your resume; they're about immersing yourself in the culture and operations of your new industry. They provide a platform to demonstrate your value, learn industry-specific skills, and build a network that can support your career transition and beyond.

By stepping up and taking on these roles, you're not just participating in your new industry - you're helping to shape it. And in doing so, you're crafting a compelling narrative of leadership and initiative that can make you an irresistible candidate in your new field.

## Turning Learning into Gold

Continuing education through professional associations and schools is a secret weapon for successful career transitions. It's not just about accumulating certificates; it's about strategically acquiring the skills, knowledge, and credibility that can catapult you into your new field.

Alex, a former retail manager eyeing a transition into human resources, joined the Society for Human Resource Management (SHRM) and discovered their comprehensive certification program. Initially daunted by the breadth of material, he committed to their SHRM-CP (Certified Professional) course. The structured learning provided him with a solid foundation in HR practices, as well as connecting him with a cohort of HR professionals. During one of the online study groups, his insights on employee engagement, drawn from his retail experience, caught the attention of a senior HR director. This connection eventually led to an entry-level HR role, where he could apply his newfound knowledge while leveraging his experience.

Professional associations offer a variety of educational formats:

1. **Certification Programs:** These comprehensive courses often culminate in industry-recognized credentials.

2. **Workshops and Seminars:** Focused, intensive learning sessions on specific topics or skills

3. **Webinars:** Convenient online sessions covering current trends and practices.

4. **Online Courses:** Self-paced learning options for flexible skill acquisition.

5. **Conferences:** Immersive events combining multiple learning formats with networking opportunities.

The power of these educational offerings lies not just in the content, but in their industry relevance and recognition. Take Maria's journey from graphic designer to UX designer. Through her membership in the User Experience Professionals Association (UXPA), she enrolled in a series of UX design workshops. These weren't just theoretical; they involved real-world projects and peer reviews. Maria's portfolio, built through these workshops, became her ticket to interviews with tech companies, effectively bridging her skills gap.

Continuing education through associations also offers the advantage of staying current in rapidly evolving fields. James, a veteran journalist transitioning to digital marketing, found the American Marketing

Association's constant stream of webinars on emerging digital trends invaluable. "It was like having a crystal ball into the industry's future," James reflected. During a job interview, his ability to discuss the latest in AI-driven marketing strategies, learned from a recent webinar, set him apart from other candidates and landed him the position.

For many, the structured nature of association-led education provides the discipline needed for a successful transition. Lisa, moving from teaching to corporate training, appreciated the accountability of her ATD (Association for Talent Development) certification program. "Having deadlines and a clear curriculum kept me focused during a time when I could have easily become overwhelmed by the career change process," she noted.

The networking aspect of these educational programs cannot be overstated. David, transitioning to sustainability consulting, found that his classmates in a green business certification course became his most valuable professional network. "We were all from different backgrounds but united in our passion for sustainability. Those connections have been crucial in my new career," David shared.

When approaching continuing education through associations:

1. **Audit your skills gap:** Identify the key areas where you need development for your target career.

2. **Research industry-valued certifications:** Some credentials carry more weight than others in specific fields. Don't accept one person's opinion. Find certifications that people agree on as important

3. **Balance immediate needs with long-term goals:** Choose a mix of quick-win workshops and longer-term certification programs.

4. **Leverage learning for networking:** Actively engage in group projects and discussions.

5. **Apply learning immediately:** Look for opportunities to put your new knowledge into practice, even in volunteer roles.

Remember, continuing education in professional associations is not just about learning; it's about transformation. It's a process of reinventing yourself professionally, gaining confidence in your new field, and building a network of peers and mentors who can support your transition.

By fully embracing these educational opportunities, you're not just preparing for a new career, you are actively involving yourself in a new professional community. You're demonstrating commitment, working to stay ahead of industry trends, and building a foundation of knowledge and connections that can support you throughout your career. This commitment to continuous learning through professional associations can be the differentiator that makes your career aspirations real.

## Navigating Job Markets Through Associations

Professional association job boards are often ways to find opportunities that elude the general public. They serve as curated marketplaces where industry-specific positions are showcased to an audience of qualified professionals. For career transitioners, these job boards are not just listings; they're places to find roles that align with your new career.

The power of association job boards lies in their exclusivity and relevance. Unlike general job sites flooded with positions across countless industries, these platforms focus solely on your chosen field. This means every listing is potentially relevant to your career transition, significantly streamlining your job search process.

Many job boards featurepositions that never make it to public job sites. Companies often prefer to recruit through professional associations to tap into a pool of candidates who are actively engaged in the industry. This means that by accessing these boards, you're privy to a hidden job market, giving you a competitive edge in your job search.

The quality of listings on association job boards frequently are higher than those on public sites. Employers posting here are often looking for people who demonstrate commitment to the field through their association membership. This can work in your favor as a career changer, signaling your serious intention to establish yourself in the new industry.

These job boards frequently offer more than just listings. Many include salary information, detailed job descriptions, and insights into company cultures that are relevant to your new field. This wealth of information can be invaluable in helping you target your applications and prepare for interviews.

Some associations go beyond passive job listings, offering proactive job alerts. They use your profile and preferences to alert you to relevant openings, ensuring you do not miss an opportunity.

To maximize the benefits of these job boards:

1. **Keep your profile up-to-date:** Ensure your association profile reflects your latest skills and career objectives.

2. **Set up job alerts:** Configure notifications for new postings that match your criteria.

3. **Research thoroughly:** Use the detailed information to tailor your applications and prepare for interviews.

4. **Network through the platform:** Many association job boards allow you to see who posted the job, and connect to company representatives and/or employees who work for the firm.

5. **Leverage your membership status:** Mention your association membership in your application and resume to demonstrate your commitment.

6. **Participate in virtual job fairs:** Many associations host online career events, providing direct access to employers.

7. **Seek application advice:** Some associations offer resume review services or application tips specific to your new industry.

8. **Use the board as a research tool:** Even if you're not actively applying, regularly reviewing listings can give you insights into industry trends and in-demand skills.

By fully utilizing association job boards, you're not just searching for a job; you're strategically positioning yourself. The job board gives you a view of your new field's job market, helping you understand where you fit and how to navigate your transition most effectively.

Remember, the true value of these job boards extends beyond the listings themselves. They're a reflection of your industry's current needs and future direction. By engaging with these platforms, you're not just finding job openings; you're gaining crucial intelligence that can inform your career transition strategy and accelerate your journey into your new professional realm.

## Try to Have a Mentor by Your Side

Mentorship programs are like having a personal tour guide for your career change. Mentors are people who've already done what you want to do and are ready to share their map and point out all the shortcuts and pitfalls. Many professional associations, not all, have figured out how to play matchmaker between seasoned pros and eager career changers like yourself.

Programs come in all shapes and sizes. Some are as formal as a black-tie dinner, with structured meeting schedules and goal-setting exercises. Others are like a casual coffee chat, where you can pick your mentor's brain over a latte. Either way, the goal is the same: to give you insider access to the wisdom, experience, and networks that can turbocharge your career transition.

Now, you might be thinking, "Why would someone want to mentor me?" Well, most professionals love sharing their knowledge. It's a chance for them to give back, reflect on their careers, and sometimes even learn from your perspective. Plus, many have been in your shoes before and remember how valuable guidance was during their career pivots.

So, what can you expect from these mentorship programs? First off, a reality check. Your mentor can help you understand the core of your new field – the unwritten rules, the skills that matter, and the challenges you might face. They're like a human FAQ for your career questions.

It's not just about getting answers; it's about expanding your thinking. A good mentor can open doors you didn't even know existed. They might invite you to industry events, introduce you to key people, or give you the inside scoop on upcoming opportunities. It can be like networking on steroids.

Here's how to make the most of a mentorship program:

1. Be clear about what you want: The more specific you are about your goals, the better your mentor can help you.

2. Come prepared: Treat each meeting like a mini-masterclass. Come with questions, ideas, and updates on your progress.

3. Be open to feedback: Sometimes, the advice you need isn't always the advice you want to hear. Listen and keep an open mind.

4. Take action: The best way to show appreciation for your mentor's time is to put their advice into practice and let them know what happened.

5. Give as well as receive: Look for ways to add value to your mentor's life too. Maybe you have skills from your current career that could be useful to them.

6. Stay in touch: If you are in a formal program, keep your mentor updated on your progress even after it ends. They'll likely be thrilled to hear from you.

Remember, a mentorship program isn't a magic wand that instantly transforms your career. It's more like an accelerator for your efforts. You still need to do the heavy lifting, but with a mentor's guidance, you'll be lifting smarter, not just harder.

So, if your professional association offers a mentorship program, jump on it like it's the last lifeboat off a sinking cruise ship. It could be the difference between doggy-paddling in your career transition and surfing the waves like a pro.

## Keep Up to Speed

Staying up-to-date is not just about being well-versed in conversation, but about strategically positioning yourself. Being well-informed is akin to having a competitive edge in your professional toolkit.

Consider your association's publications, newsletters, and industry journals as strategic foresight tools. These resources are your conduit to understanding industry dynamics and anticipating trends – invaluable skills for your next professional interaction or interview.

Association publications offer an insider's perspective on your new industry. They typically contain in-depth analyses, upcoming event information, and profiles of industry leaders. Make these a priority in your professional reading.

Newsletters provide concise, timely updates on industry developments. They're like executive summaries of what's current in your new field. A practical approach is to create a dedicated folder in your email inbox and create a rule to deliver them there. This allows for efficient access when you want to quickly refresh your thoughts and knowledge before a networking event or interview.

Industry journals represent the pinnacle of in-depth information. While they may initially seem complex, regular engagement with these publications will significantly enhance your industry-specific knowledge. Consistent reading will enable you to confidently discuss ideas, advanced concepts, and current trends as if you've been in the industry for years.

Here are strategies to effectively stay informed:

1. **Establish a routine:** Create dedicated time daily for industry updates. Treat it as part of your professional development.

2. **Leverage technology:** Use tools like Google Alerts for key terms to streamline information gathering.

3. **Engage with thought leaders**: Follow industry experts on professional social media platforms for real-time insights.

4. **Participate in professional forums:** Engage in online discussions to gain diverse perspectives on industry topics.

5. **Maintain a trend log:** Document key insights and emerging patterns. This can be valuable material for interviews and networking.

6. **Share your knowledge:** Disseminate relevant information within your network to establish yourself as an engaged professional.

7. **Apply insights practically:** Think about how new information can be applied to your job search or current role.

The objective is not to become an exhaustive repository of industry information but to develop a nuanced understanding of your new field. It's about gaining the ability to engage in informed discussions, comprehend current challenges, and identify emerging opportunities.

By immersing yourself in these publications, approaching newsletters as valuable industry updates, and tackling journals as opportunities for deep learning, you'll rapidly transition from an industry newcomer to a well-informed professional.

## Forge Your Professional Edge:

Professional development is the cornerstone of career evolution, particularly for those navigating a transition. It's not just about adding credentials to your resume; it's about sculpting yourself into the professional your new industry demands. Let's explore how leveraging these opportunities can transform your career trajectory, illustrated by the experiences of two successful career pivoters.

Professional associations offer a smorgasbord of development options:

1. **Workshops:** Intensive, hands-on sessions focusing on specific skills or topics.

2. **Seminars:** Broader, often lecture-style events covering industry trends and best practices.

3. **Certification Programs:** Structured courses leading to recognized industry credentials.

4. **Webinars**: Online sessions offering flexibility and often covering cutting-edge topics.

5. **Conferences:** Immersive events combining multiple learning formats with networking.

Olive was a former marketing executive transitioning into environmental sustainability. After joining the International Society of Sustainability Professionals, she discovered their Sustainability Excellence Associate certification. This program not only provided her with a solid foundation in sustainability practices but also introduced her to a cohort of like-minded people. During a group project, Olive's innovative approach to corporate sustainability reporting caught the attention of another participant, who happened to be a hiring manager at a green tech firm. This connection, coupled with her newly acquired certification, led to a position that bridged her marketing expertise with her passion for sustainability.

The value of professional development extends beyond any knowledge gained. It demonstrates a commitment to your new field and can often be the differentiator in a competitive job market. Ray, a software engineer pivoting to healthcare technology, enrolled in a series of workshops on healthcare data through his membership in the Healthcare Information and Management Systems Society (HIMSS).

These sessions not only equipped him with industry-specific knowledge but also provided hands-on experience with healthcare-specific software systems. During an interview for a health tech startup, Ray's ability to discuss real-world applications of data analytics in healthcare settings, learned from these workshops, set him apart from other candidates with more traditional tech backgrounds.

To maximize professional development opportunities:

1. **Conduct a skills gap analysis:** Identify key areas where you need development for your target career.

2. **Research industry-valued certifications:** Some credentials carry more weight in specific fields.

3. **Balance immediate needs with long-term goals:** Choose a mix of quick-win workshops and longer-term certification programs. Quick wins help you build up endurance and a feeling of accomplishment.

4. **Apply learning immediately:** Look for opportunities to put your new knowledge into practice, even in volunteer roles.

5. **Network actively during these events:** Engage with instructors and fellow participants.

Remember, professional development in the context of career transition is not just about learning; it's about transformation. It's a process of reinventing yourself professionally, gaining confidence in your new field, and building a network of peers and mentors who can support your transition.

By fully embracing these development opportunities, you're not just preparing for a new career; you're actively participating in your new professional community. You're demonstrating commitment, staying ahead of industry trends, and building a foundation of knowledge and connections that can support you throughout your career journey.

In the landscape of career transitions, this commitment to continuous learning and professional development can be the catalyst that turns your career aspirations into tangible opportunities. It's about equipping yourself with the tools, knowledge, and networks to not only enter your new field, but to thrive and excel.

# Collaborating Your Way into a New Career

Collaborative projects offer a unique blend of hands-on experience, networking opportunities, and industry exposure that can catapult your transition from aspiration to reality.

Professional associations typically offer various collaborative opportunities:

1. **Research Initiatives:** In-depth studies on industry trends or challenges.

2. **Community Outreach Projects:** Efforts to apply industry expertise to social causes.

3. **White Paper Development**: Collaborative authorship of industry thought leadership pieces

4. **Technology Pilots:** Testing and implementing new industry-specific technologies.

5. **Policy Development:** Contributing to industry standards or regulatory recommendations.

The beauty of these projects lies in their ability to immerse you in real-world industry scenarios while expanding your professional network. They're like mini internships but with the added benefit of working alongside established professionals.

Consider the journey of Perry, transitioning into corporate learning and development volunteered for a research project examining the impact of gamification on adult learning after joining the Association for Talent Development (ATD). Despite her limited corporate experience, her background in education proved invaluable to the team. The project not only allowed Perry to apply her teaching expertise in a new context but also exposed her to cutting-edge L&D practices. During the project's presentation at an ATD conference, Perry's insights caught the attention of a senior L&D director from a Fortune 500 company. This connection led to a role that beautifully merged her educational background with corporate training needs.

Collaborative projects can also be powerful catalysts for innovation and career differentiation. For example, Leo, a financial analyst venturing into sustainable investing participated in a working group developing guidelines for ESG (Environmental, Social, and Governance) integration in investment analysis. He volunteered for a research project examining the impact of gamification on adult learning. This project not only deepened his understanding of sustainable finance but also positioned him as a contributor to emerging industry standards. During a job interview with a socially responsible investment firm, Leo's ability to discuss the nuances of ESG integration, backed by his hands-on experience from the project, set him apart as a candidate who wasn't just interested in sustainable investing but was actively shaping its future.

To maximize collaborative project opportunities:

1. **Make sure they align with your goals:** Choose projects that develop skills or provide experiences relevant to your target career.

2. **Leverage your existing expertise:** Look for ways to apply your previous career skills in new contexts.

3. **Be proactive**: Volunteer for leadership roles within the project team.

4. **Document your contributions:** Keep a detailed record of your work for your portfolio and future interviews.

5. **Network strategically:** Build relationships with team members and use the project as a conversation starter in industry events.

Remember, collaborative projects in professional associations are more than just resume builders. They're opportunities to demonstrate your value, learn industry-specific skills, and build a network that can support your career transition and beyond. They allow you to contribute meaningfully to your new field even before you've officially "arrived."

By actively engaging in these collaborative initiatives, you're not just preparing for a new career; you're already participating in it. You're building a bridge between your past expertise and your future aspirations, creating a narrative of continuous growth and adaptability that can be incredibly compelling to potential employers.

In the landscape of career transitions, collaborative projects can be the difference between telling potential employers what you could do and showing them what you've already accomplished. They're your opportunity to write the first chapter of your new career story, surrounded by supportive characters invested in your success.

**Amplify Your Voice**

Leveraging your memberships effectively can significantly enhance your professional profile during a career transition. These affiliations can catch the eye of potential employers when strategically showcased. Create a "Professional Affiliations" section near the top of your resume. This placement immediately signals to recruiters and hiring managers your engagement with the industry. Don't simply list names; provide context:

- Highlight leadership roles or committee positions
- Mention specific projects or initiatives you've contributed to
- Note any awards or recognition received through the association

Your LinkedIn profile is another place to showcase memberships. Use the "Organizations" section, and also integrate them into your professional summary. For instance, "Active member of [Association Name], contributing to industry-wide initiatives" succinctly demonstrates your involvement.

Maximize your LinkedIn presence by:

- Creating posts or articles that showcase insights from association events

- Discussing industry trends learned through your membership

- Highlighting collaborative projects you're part of through the association Share links to articles from the association as well as others that demonstrate interesting ideas

Engage actively on LinkedIn:

- Comment on and share posts from your associations
- Connect with fellow members and participate in meaningful discussions
- Join and contribute to association-sponsored LinkedIn groups

Key strategies for leveraging your memberships:

1. **Be selective:** Highlight memberships most relevant to your target career

2. Stay active: Regularly update your involvement and achievements

3. **Connect the dots:** Clearly explain how your memberships relate to your career goals

4. **Use keywords:** Include industry-specific terms associated with your memberships and new career

5. **Tell a story:** Use your memberships to craft a narrative of your career transition journey

Your association memberships are more than just credentials. They signal your professional trajectory and can serve as conversation starters in interviews. By strategically highlighting these affiliations, you demonstrate that you're an engaged, informed, and committed member of your new professional community.

In the competitive landscape of career transitions, your association memberships can be the differentiator that moves your application from consideration to action. They show potential employers that you're not just looking for a job in a new field, but you're already an active participant in that professional world.

Remember, the goal is to use memberships to create a compelling narrative of your transition, showcasing your proactive approach to entering and contributing to your new field. When leveraged effectively, these affiliations can open doors, spark meaningful conversations, and ultimately help you transition.

Joining professional associations is a strategic investment in your career transition journey, but the true value emerges through active engagement and strategic utilization of available resources. Your membership opens doors to a vast network of professionals and events that can lead to interactions, learning opportunities, job leads, and jobs. Many industries fill positions through networking before public advertising them, making these connections invaluable.

Take full advantage of educational resources like webinars, workshops, and conferences. These aren't just learning opportunities; they're chances to stay ahead of industry trends and demonstrate your commitment to professional growth. Many associations offer skill-building programs or certifications that can be crucial in bridging gaps between your previous career and your new field. Prioritize those highly regarded in your target industry.

Volunteer for committees or special projects within the association to build skills and increase your visibility. Leadership roles in association activities can significantly boost your professional profile. Use members-only resources such as industry reports, salary surveys, and job boards for valuable insights in your job search and career planning.

Seize the opportunity if the association offers a mentorship program. A mentor established in your target field can provide invaluable guidance, insider knowledge, and potentially open doors to opportunities. Consider contributing articles to association publications or blogs. This can establish you as a thoughtful contributor to your new field, even as you're transitioning into it.

Take advantage of any career services offered such as resume reviews or career counseling. These services, tailored to your specific industry, can be valuable in positioning yourself effectively for your new career. Regularly reassess how you're using your membership and look for new ways to engage (more). As you progress in your transition, your needs may change, and different aspects of the association may become more relevant.

Periodically evaluate the return on your membership investment, considering factors like new skills acquired, connections made, job leads generated, and how membership has enhanced your professional brand. Remember, a professional association membership is not a passive credential; it's an active platform for growth, networking, and opportunity creation. The more you engage, the more value you'll derive.

As you progress in your new field, consider how to give back to others. Mentoring newcomers, leading workshops, or contributing to association initiatives can further cement your position in your new industry while helping others with their careers.

Association memberships can be a powerful tool in your career transition toolkit. By fully leveraging its resources, actively participating in its community, and consistently seeking ways to learn and contribute, you transform your membership from a simple professional affiliation into a dynamic catalyst for your career evolution. Your engagement with the association becomes a testament to your commitment, a platform for your growth, and a launchpad for your success in your new professional realm. The investment you make in joining and actively participating in professional associations can significantly accelerate your journey into a new field, providing access to a network of professionals, resources, and invaluable opportunities.

# Epilogue To Sum Up

Embarking on a career change is a journey that demands both patience and unwavering persistence. It's a path that goes far beyond finding a new job; instead, it's about discovering a professional trajectory that truly resonates with your innermost passions and sense of purpose. This alignment between your work and your authentic self is the key to unlocking greater fulfillment and satisfaction in your professional life.

The career transition process can often feel overwhelming, which is why having a structured approach can be invaluable. This step-by-step guide provides a roadmap, helping you navigate the complexities of this change. However, it's important to remember that everyone's career journey is unique. While this advice and these guidelines can be helpful, you'll ultimately need to chart the course that feels right for your circumstances and goals.

Self-assessment forms the foundation of a successful transition. Take the time to deeply understand your skills, values, and interests. This self-knowledge will guide you as you research potential new career paths. An investigation is crucial before making any significant moves.

Networking usually plays a pivotal role in transitions, often opening doors you might not have known existed. Don't hesitate to connect with professionals in your target field. These connections can provide invaluable insights and opportunities.

As you progress, you may identify gaps in your qualifications. Embrace these as opportunities for growth and look for ways to develop the skills you need. Remember, setbacks are a natural part of any significant change. Try to view challenges as learning experiences that will ultimately contribute to your success.

For some, a gradual transition may be more feasible than an abrupt change. Consider making a series of smaller moves that build towards your ultimate goal. Volunteering and/or looking for ways to do work on the side can lead to experience that will help you make your change. Doing this will help mitigate risks and allow for adjustment along the way.

Financial planning is an often-overlooked aspect of career transitions. Be prepared for the possibility of a period of reduced income and plan accordingly. This foresight can provide peace of mind as you navigate your change.

While self-guided resources like books and articles can be extremely helpful, some individuals may benefit from more personalized support. Career coaches like me can offer tailored advice, help you overcome obstacles, and provide accountability during your transition. However, it's important to carefully consider whether paid coaching aligns with your needs and budget before making that investment.

Ultimately, changing careers is a significant decision that requires careful thought and planning. However, with the right approach and mindset, it can lead to a more fulfilling and authentic professional life. Trust in your ability to navigate this change, and remember that the effort you make is often as rewarding as the destination.

# More from Jeff Altman

If you join JobSearch.Community as any level of Insider, you receive access to all of my video courses, books and guides for one monthly price. That includes these books and guides which are all available individually on Amazon:

The Right Answers to Tough Interview Questions
The Ultimate Job Interview Framework (a terrific guide to how to interview better than your competition)
101 Ways to Find Job Leads
Background Checks: What Are They Trying to Find Out
No BS Questions You Should Ask on Any Interview
3 Great Ways to Answer Tell Me About Yourself
Great Answers to Behavioral Interview Questions
Final Interview Preparation

How to Avoid Being Laid Off, Excessed, RIFd, Furloughed or Made Redundant. The following are free at JobSearch.Community and for a small amount on Amazon:

No BS Resume Advice
Diagnosing Your Job Search Problems
Get Ready for the Job Jungle (how to start a job search)
25 Job Interview Questions and Answers


All of my video courses are also available for the same membership price at JobSearch.Community or individually at www.TheBigGameHunter.us/courses They are available to rent or buy except where marked.

The Ultimate Job Interview Framework video course
Salary Negotiation Mistakes to Avoid
Start Your New Job Like a Star
Final Interview Preparation video course
Informational Interviews

The Top 10 Questions to Prepare for on Every Interview PLUS Bonuses

More Answers to Tough Interview Questions (buy only)
Salary Negotiation Tactics
Cover Letters That Get Results  (buy only)
Job Interview Preparation

www.ingramcontent.com/pod-product-compliance
Lightning Source LLC
Chambersburg PA
CBHW071916210526
45479CB00002B/438